THE SEVEN RAYS
MADE VISUAL

THE SEVEN RAYS
MADE VISUAL

An Illustrated Introduction to the Teaching on
the Seven Rays
of Djwhal Khul and Alice A. Bailey

Helen S. Burmester

DeVORSS & Co., *Publishers*
P. O. Box 550
Marina del Rey, CA 90294

The teachings on the Seven Rays provide a key to a preliminary understanding of the Divine Plan of Creation on cosmic, solar, planetary, human, and subhuman levels, and of our place in the scheme as a whole. It is a holistic approach, a synthesis of invisible and visible worlds.

Contents

Preface

The usual concept of energy does not account for its having quality or consciousness. Only recently has science come to the point of including qualities such as intelligence, goodwill, and love as characteristics of energy. The concept of the Seven Rays is not new with *A Treatise on the Seven Rays*[1]; it has been explored before, but important, new, and promising information—especially for psychology—has been offered. This is what we are trying to understand, for each human being (as well as other units of conscious life) is born with an individual pattern of attunement. No two are alike. The ebb and flow of the seven ray energies affect all units of consciousness in different ways, resulting in the great diversity within the One Life.

Another way in which the concept of the Seven Rays differs from the conventional attitude towards energy can be seen in the hylozoistic viewpoint, namely, wherever there is a unit of matter, there is also a unit of conscious life, whether it be an atom, a human being, a planet, or a galaxy.[2]

Interest in what lies behind our visible and invisible worlds prompted me to attempt, in visual form and greatly simplified terms, an introduction to the fascinating teachings on the Seven Rays by Djwhal Khul as given to Alice A. Bailey in five volumes of *A Treatise on the Seven Rays* and other books, published by Lucis Trust, New York.

These seven great Ray-Lives are the expression of Divinity and are the builders of all that exists in space. The primary concern in this teaching is the evolution of consciousness within the various kingdoms of nature, of which there are seven—three below the human, the human, and three above the human kingdom.

In our present solar system the evolution of consciousness begins in the mineral kingdom and is extended in the vegetable and animal kingdoms. It finds its greater unfoldment in the human kingdom and its greatest unfoldment in the three kingdoms above the human—that of the Soul, the Spirit or Monad, and of Divinity. Its many implications for, and relationships to, planetary, solar, and cosmic consciousness open up tremendous vistas of the ONE in Whom we live and move and have our being.

Knowing that the extension and development of consciousness does not stop with the human kingdom but expands with ever greater inclusiveness and understanding into cosmic realms, into the Glory of the ONE, it is hoped that this modest introduction will entice the reader to study more deeply, especially the *Treatise on the Seven Rays*, which consists of:

Volumes I, II: *Esoteric Psychology*

Volume III: *Esoteric Astrology*

Volume IV: *Esoteric Healing*

Volume V: *The Rays and the Initiations*

Thanks to the Master Teacher's dispensation, we can gain a deep and significant insight into these radiating streams of energy and their influences on our planet, on humanity as a whole, and on each individual human life. Though their origin and source of potency go far beyond the zodiacal constellations to cosmic sources, these seven great Ray-Lives are responsible for the evolution of consciousness and form from their very beginning in the atom. The idea of a distant God disappears.

We know from scientific research that even an atom, which is invisible to our unaided eye, is a potential world. So, by analogy, we may assume that a human being, as a composite of trillions of physical, emotional, and mental atoms, is a potential solar system, and that humanity, with its sixty billion units in and out of incarnation, is a potential galaxy.

Each unit of life is part of a greater life. It evolves in form and consciousness from an atom to a cell, a molecule, an organ, an organism all the way through the mineral, vegetable, and animal kingdoms to the human, and from there to ever greater inclusiveness, power, and beauty. This consciousness expansion is the result of the activities of the great rays of the divine septenate, which function cyclically and in various degrees throughout the universe.

Every living entity is endowed with a certain degree of consciousness or intelligence. In the human being, consciousness develops into self-consciousness, then soul-consciousness, and eventually into God-consciousness. We human beings have the innate capacity to reach up to and experience cosmic consciousness in full awareness because we are potentially a self-conscious spark of divinity. We are a magnificent, incredible conglomeration of physical, emotional, and mental units of life that form our personality, which in turn is the vehicle for our consciousness, or soul; and the soul is the vehicle for the spirit, the spark of divinity, God immanent.

As we strive toward this cosmic consciousness and oneness with all, veil after veil falls off that hides our innate essential divinity, our Christ-consciousness, our true Self, which is ever trying to reveal itself under the influences of the seven great Rays that function on cosmic, solar, and planetary levels. They are transmitted from cosmic sources through the zodiacal constellations to our Sun with its planets, to our Earth, and to each unit of life on earth. The vastness of space in which we live is alive, vibrating, singing, permeating our very being with the joy and beauty of spirit if we are sensitive and receptive to it.

Many readers are probably well acquainted with astrological terminology, with the interpretation of zodiacal influences, and with the effects of planetary forces on human life. But behind and beyond and coming through the Zodiac and our solar system are the seven streams of divine energy, the Seven Rays, which emanate on cosmic levels from the Most High, the Absolute. In the process of manifestation, creation, and evolution, these Seven Rays express and transmit the qualities, characteristics, and purpose of the Absolute, but each Ray has its own characteristics, quality, and purpose as well.

These Rays are the seven great builders of all that exists—from universes, galaxies, solar systems down to the subatomic level of protons, neutrons, and electrons. Their tremendous scope and interrelating network of energies and forces present a holistic approach and a synthesis of invisible and visible worlds. And it is the potent cyclic playing of the seven ray energies upon manifested life that produces the complex problems in national and international affairs as well as in our personal lives.

Where and how did these powerful rays come into being? The ultimate source or origin of the Seven Rays is the Absolute, the all-inclusive Whole, to which all else is relative. This absolute Being experiences within Itself on cosmic levels the first differentiation into a Trinity of Father, Son, and Holy Ghost: Three in One or One in Three. Then, during the process of manifestation, we get to know this Trinity on lower levels as reflections in the *three Rays of Aspect*: The Father aspect as *Ray I of Will or Power*; the son aspect as *Ray II of Love-Wisdom*, or the cosmic Christ Who descends into the lower regions with His divine message; and the Holy Ghost as *Ray III of Active Intelligence*. These three Qualities permeate all that exists.

The other day I came across an interesting statement by Albert Szent-Györgyi, a Nobel Prize-winning biochemist. In his book *The Physical Basis of Life*, he says that "the best scientists of today, with the aid of giant computers, cannot yet fully explain the behavior of three electrons moving within an atom. Yet those three electrons . . . know exactly what to do and never miss."[3] It made me think of the Trinity within the Absolute, which may be reflected even in as small a unit as an atom.

The second differentiation of the Logos brought forth, in addition to the three Rays of Aspect, the four Rays of Attribute, which demonstrate the qualities of the rays of aspect in greater detail. They are:

Ray IV, the Ray of Harmony through Conflict

Ray V, the Ray of Concrete Knowledge or Science

Ray VI, the Ray of Idealism and Devotion

Ray VII, the Ray of Ceremonial Magic and Order

These four Rays of Attribute are synthesised in the third Ray of Aspect, the Ray of Active Intelligence.

These most powerful entities function on cosmic levels throughout the vastness of space in every solar system. Our Sun, for instance, is on the second cosmic Ray of Love-Wisdom, and the seven rays that function in our solar system are seven sub-rays of this Ray of Love-Wisdom. However, even in their lesser potency, their characteristics, their quality, and their purpose are the same as those of their cosmic prototypes. It is a fascinating story of interrelated energies and their effect on human life and on all that lives. And what responds to these various ray energies is our own true Self, our soul, our Christ-consciousness within. God immanent and God transcendent are ever-present realities and permeate all that exists. Our sensitivity to these radiating energies and forces determines our consciousness development and the degree to which we become consciously aware of the tremendous universe of which we are a living part, endowed potentially with all the glorious possibilities of expanding into the realm of the divine.

It is interesting to know that these cosmic, solar, and planetary energies become forces when applied to our life or to the various kingdoms of nature. Both energies and forces are essentially neutral and depend for their effectiveness for good or bad on the spiritual development of a person, a nation, or humanity as a whole. We respond according to the state of our own development in consciousness.

Behind each Ray stands a great Cosmic Being to Whom we give the name of "Lord of a Ray." Each human being belongs by nature to a particular Ray but will also include the other six ray types. D. K. tells us that "there is nothing in the whole solar system, at whatever stage of evolution it may stand, which does not belong and has not always belonged to one or other of the Seven Rays."[4]

NOTES

1. Alice A. Bailey, *A Treatise on the Seven Rays* (New York: Lucis Trust).
2. Alice A. Bailey, *A Treatise on Cosmic Fire* (New York: Lucis Trust), p. 693.
3. Albert Szent-Györgyi, *The Physical Basis of Life* (CRM Books), p. xi.
4. Alice A. Bailey, *Esoteric Psychology* I, p. 163.

THE SEVEN RAYS
MADE VISUAL

I. OF THIS *ULTIMATE REALITY*, EACH LIVING BEING IS AN IN-
FINITESIMAL SPARK, WORKING, WITH EVER EXPANDING AWARENESS,
ITS WAY BACK TO THE SOURCE.

I Ultimate Reality

There is but one ultimate reality. It exists beyond our vision and comprehension. All else is relative to It. And there is little we can know about the Absolute. Therefore a pure white disc and a golden circle without beginning or end may serve as a symbol for the Absolute.

In *A Treatise on Cosmic Fire* we read: "There is one Boundless Immutable Principle; one Absolute Reality which antecedes all manifested conditioned Being. It is beyond the range and reach of any human thought or expression."[1]

Within this Absolute Reality is contained all life, which, once it has become manifest, we can perceive as countless galaxies, stars, and solar systems. Each of these Cosmic Entities is the manifestation of the energy of a Great Life within which further differentiations take place. Lesser units come forth, evolve, and return, just as in our solar system, on our Planet Earth, units of divine life appear as human beings. They grow, evolve, become at last fully conscious on all levels, and return to their source.

In some excerpts of Manly P. Hall's mystical poetry we hear the Absolute speaking of Himself:

> I am the Absolute. I am birthless,
> > Deathless, eternal;
> The baseless Base of Beginnings,
> > The sure Foundation unmeasured,
> The causeless Cause of Causation,
> > The Living Root of Illusion.
>
> All these am I, and other things
> > Unmentioned;
> The sum total of Reality expressed
> > In Naught;
> Unmoved, unquestioned, undefined:
> > I am Omnipotent.

Veiled by the robes of empty space,
    I dream
The troubled nightmare of Creation's Plan,
    To wake
and find Creation's Plan dissolved again
    In Me . . .

Of Me you little know, and yet
    Am I the sum
Of all that has been, is,
    Or yet to come—
The Plan, the Planner and the Planned-for
    All in one . . .

I am the Absolute;
    I, the One before the beginning . . .
The Word unspoken is my Name;
    I am the All-Pervading.[2]

NOTES

1. *A Treatise on Cosmic Fire*, p. 3.
2. Manly Palmer Hall, *The Space Born* (Philosophical Research Society), pp. 7–9.

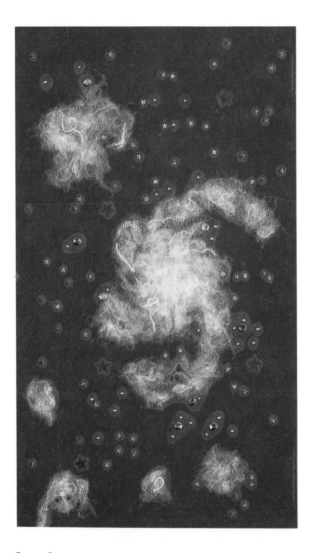

II. THE *ONE LIFE* MANIFESTS IN COUNTLESS UNIVERSES, SOLAR SYSTEMS, PLANETS, HUMAN BEINGS, AND IN ANYTHING THAT LIVES.

The huge 200-inch Hale reflector on Mount Palomar in California—the world's largest working optical telescope—can see as many as a million galaxies inside the bowl of the Big Dipper alone. Astronomers believe that the star we call our Sun was "born" about five billion years ago and may change little for its next five billion years. (See *National Geographic*, May 1974.)

II   Manifestation of the ONE

When this Most High decided to manifest His "nightmare of creation," He began to express Himself in myriads of forms such as:

Universes	Human Beings
Galaxies	Animals
Constellations	Trees and Flowers
Solar Systems	Minerals
Planets	Atoms

all of which are living entities that fill the cosmic expanse with their radiations and create a tremendous interrelated network of energies and forces. And all of it serves the purpose of bringing back to the Father's House the sparks of divinity that were, and will be, sent out and, returned home, are fully aware and enriched by their experiences and their creative expressions. The process of creation seems to be in operation continuously, for stars are "born" and "die," and their number is endless.

In the teaching on the Seven Rays, which permeates all of his writings, the Master Djwhal Khul is primarily concerned with the development of consciousness within the human kingdom, to help each of its members to proceed from the fourth kingdom—the human—to the fifth kingdom of nature, to that of the soul and spirit.

It is difficult to express in words the significance of the development of such an elusive concept as that of consciousness. What is consciousness? How can it be developed? If consciousness serves as a synonym for soul, we must first become fully and consciously aware of our own divinity within, and of the essential divinity in all that lives, before we can consciously tune into the streams of divine energies and forces that surround us, permeate our very being, and impel us to reveal that innate splendour, which is our own true Self. This inner core knows the divine purpose and intent, and as we become aware of this magnificent reality, we begin to see how the whole story of creation and evolution is the expression and realisation of the Plan of God.

7

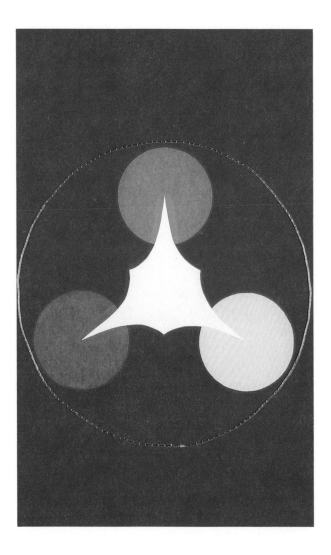

III. *THE ONE DIFFERENTIATES INTO THREE*: THE THREE GREAT
RAYS OF ASPECT.

All divisions are, of course, unreal and only serve the purpose of intelligent understanding.

III   Three Rays of Aspect

The first differentiation within the Absolute—of the ONE into Three—was experienced on cosmic levels before manifestation took place and resulted in the Trinity of Father, Son, and Holy Ghost. When Spirit and Matter united, the Soul or Consciousness was born.

In a Treatise on the Seven Rays we find various designations for the Holy Trinity:

Spirit	or *Monad*	or *Life*	or *Father*
Consciousness	*Soul*	*Quality*	*Son*
Matter	*Body*	*Appearance*	*Holy Ghost*

In the processes of manifestation, this threefold Unity expresses Itself in the Great Rays of Aspect, which are:

Ray I	*Ray II*	*Ray III*
(red)	*(blue)*	(yellow)
Will or Power	*Love-Wisdom*	*Active-Intelligence*

These three major rays constitute the sum total of the entire divine manifestation. They are active in every form of life. Through the activity of these creative agencies of God, every form is imbued with that inner evolutionary attribute which must eventually sweep it into line with divine purpose and fulfill its destiny as a corporate part of the whole.[1]

We may ask, what is a Ray? A Ray is but a name for a particular force or type of energy, with the emphasis upon the quality which that force exhibits and not upon the form aspect that it creates.

Divisions and categories are *not* separations, because all life is one—one organism, in which every cell plays its part. But these divisions help us to understand more clearly and intelligently the issues involved.

9

While we cannot express Life nor its perfection in words as yet, we can understand somewhat the process of "becoming" which leads to "being." With it, the expression that "Matter is spirit at the lowest point of its cyclic activity and spirit is matter at its highest point" becomes more than just an intellectual statement in our thinking.

These three Rays of Aspect on the cosmic level are as much of a mystery to our finite understanding as is the Absolute Himself. But, thanks to the teaching of our Tibetan Master who brings these awe-inspiring realities down to the level of our solar system, as well as to planetary and human levels, our insight expands tremendously when delving into his writings.

NOTES

1. See *Esoteric Psychology* I, pp. 149–59, 316.

IV. *OMNIPRESENCE OF THE RAYS OF ASPECT*. THESE THREE RAYS OF ASPECT, WHICH ARE WILL-TO-GOOD, LOVE-WISDOM, ACTIVE IN-TELLIGENCE OR LIGHT, PERMEATE ALL THAT EXISTS IN THE VASTNESS OF SPACE.

A Ray is but a name for a particular type of energy or divine quality.

IV   Omnipresence of the Rays of Aspect

Ray I, The Lord of Will or Power, is a Life that wills to love and that uses power as an expression of divine beneficence. The Lord of Power and Will performs the task of destruction of forms so that the manifestation of Deity may grow in power and beauty and thereby bring the revelation of God's will and beneficent purpose into being. This Lord is the controller of the death-drama in all kingdoms, which brings about release of power and permits "entrance into Light." Symbolically, Ray I embodies the dynamic idea of God, and thus the Most High starts the work of creation.

Ray II, The Lord of Love-Wisdom, is the embodiment of pure love. This Life instils into all forms the quality of love. Symbolically, this Lord of the second Ray is occupied with formulating the Plan upon which the forms must be constructed and the dynamic idea of God materialised. He is the Master Builder.

Ray III, The Lord of Active Intelligence, is more closely linked with matter. He works in cooperation with the Lord of the second Ray and constitutes the active building force that starts the work of construction and eventually materialises the idea and purpose of God.

Yet these three Rays are as much a unity as is a human being who conceives an idea, uses his mind and brain to bring the idea into manifestation, and employs his hands and all his natural forces to perfect the idea.[1] The interplay and interrelation of all three rays is synthetic on all levels—cosmic, solar, planetary, human, atomic—throughout the created universe.

NOTES

1. See *Esoteric Psychology* I, pp. 159–63.

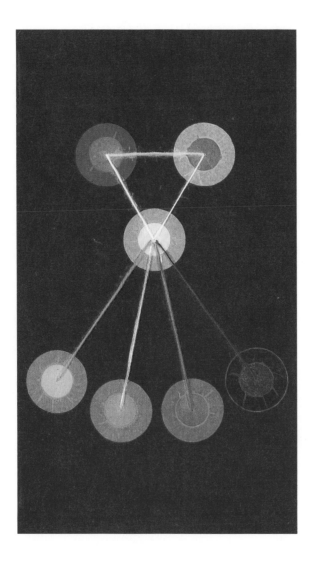

V. *FOUR RAYS OF ATTRIBUTE*. THE THREE-IN-ONE DIFFERENTIATE INTO SEVEN RADIANT QUALITIES, ADDING FOUR RAYS OF ATTRIBUTE THAT EXPRESS THE QUALITIES OF THE THREE RAYS OF ASPECT IN GREATER DETAIL.

14

V Four Rays of Attribute

The three in ONE differentiate into seven

Seven Rays, or
Seven Radiant Qualities, or
Seven Streams of Energy

which "carry into Light" the seven types of souls. They are the medium through which the three major Rays express their divine qualities. They are the sum total of the divine consciousness of the Universal Mind and might be regarded as seven intelligent Entities through Whom the divine Plan is working out. They embody divine purpose, express the qualities required for materialising that purpose, and create the forms through which the divine idea can be carried forward to completion. These seven streams of energy produce cyclically the manifested world and cooperate intelligently with the Plan of which They are the custodians.

The first three rays are *Rays of Aspect,* and the remaining four are *Rays of Attribute.* The latter find their synthesis in the third Ray of Aspect. These four Rays of Attribute produce the qualities of the three Rays of Aspect in greater detail.

In relation to man, all human monads carried into manifestation by the will and desire of some Ray-Lord are part of His body of manifestation. They express His quality, but as yet only potentially. The hidden qualities must be brought out of latency.

The four Rays of Attribute are:

RAY IV	*RAY V*	*RAY VI*	*RAY VII*
orange	green	purple	indigo
THE LORD OF HARMONY THROUGH CONFLICT	THE LORD OF SCIENCE AND CONCRETE KNOWLEDGE	THE LORD OF DEVOTION AND IDEALISM	THE LORD OF ORDER AND CEREMONIAL MAGIC

Ray IV (orange), The Ray of Harmony, Beauty, and Art

Its function is the creation of beauty through the interplay of life and form, basing the design of beauty upon the divine Plan. Its keynote is Harmony through Conflict, harmony between the desires of the form and the desires of the indwelling life. Its purpose lies in producing at-one-ment, unity, harmony, and beauty in line with divine intent. The fourth Ray is essentially a healing force, as it brings all forms to an ultimate perfection through the power of the inner life.

Ray V (green), The Lord of Concrete Knowledge and Science

This great Life is in close touch with the creative Deity. It is a Being of the intensest spiritual light through its quality of higher mind. It is a pure channel for the divine will. In this fifth Ray, love and mind must eventually and naturally reveal each other. The energies and forces illuminate the forms and reveal their inner purpose, and all is seen as rhythm.

Ray VI (purple), The Lord of Devotion and Idealism

This solar Deity is a peculiar and characteristic expression of the quality of our Solar Logos and a true and vital expression of divine nature. A militant focussing upon the ideal, a one-pointed devotion to the intent of the life-urge, and a divine sincerity are the qualities of this Lord that impress all that is found within His body of manifestation.

Ray VII (indigo), The Lord of Ceremonial Order or Magic

This Lord has a peculiar power on Earth and on the physical plane of manifestation. He is the most active one in this world period. He builds through the power of thought and makes a person delight in "all things done decently and in order."[1]

When we speak of ray energy we are in reality considering the quality and the will-purpose aspect of a certain great Life to Whom we give the name "Lord of a Ray." His divine intention, will, purpose (or the determined projection of His mind) create a radiation or stream of energy that—according to type and quality—plays upon all forms of manifested life, including our planet Earth. These Lords of the Rays are the creating and sustaining energies that implement the Will of the planetary Logos. They cooperate with Him on the definition and expression of His supreme purpose. Their radiating emanations are cyclically objectified and cyclically withdrawn.

As they radiate forth into the three worlds, the impacting energies produce changes, disturbances, progress, and unfoldment. They create the needed new forms and vitalize and qualify that through which the immediate divine intention is expressing itself. They intensify both the quality and the receptivity of "consciousness." When they withdraw, they cause cessation and dying out of form aspects, institutions, and "organising organisms." They produce cycles of destruction and cessation to make room for those new forms and life expressions that an incoming Ray will produce. (At present the sixth Ray is withdrawing and the seventh Ray is coming in.)[2]

The three Rays of Aspect and the four Rays of Attribute have their origin in the second person of the Trinity. They are the sevenfold expression of the Cosmic Christ.[3]

NOTES

1. See *Esoteric Psychology* I, pp. 59, 205–10.
2. *The Rays and the Initiations*, pp. 568–69.
3. *Esoteric Psychology* I, p. 119.

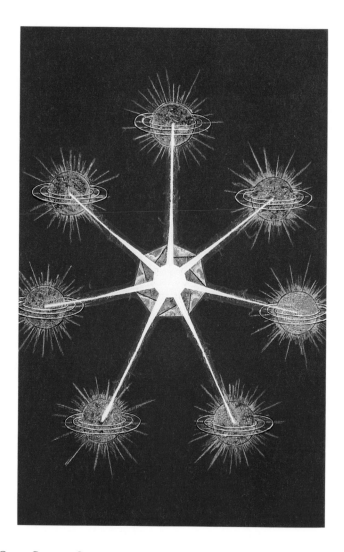

VI. *Our Solar System Is But One of Seven Solar Systems* SYNTHESIZED BY THE "ONE ABOUT WHOM NAUGHT MAY BE SAID," WHO IN TURN IS BUT AN INTEGRAL PART OF A STILL GREATER LIFE, FOR ALL LIFE EXISTS WITHIN THE ONE.

VI   Seven Solar Systems

There are *seven solar systems*, of which ours is one, and they form a great cosmic unity into which pour energies coming from certain great constellations, all of which are part of the all-pervading unity and synthesis existing in space. It has been stated that septenates of energy are, in the inner government of our particular solar system, an unalterable rule. Influences of some of these cosmic entities to which these seven solar systems belong find their way into our planetary life and produce definite effects upon the individual human being and humanity as a whole.[1]

The ONE, the Rays, Life, human beings—all are psychological entities and builders of forms. In order to manifest the qualities of the ONE, the seven great Ray-Lives gathered in space the substance they needed to express their innate quality and built it into form and appearances. Thus appeared the Heavenly Bodies:

Solar Systems
Planetary Systems
Our Earth
All Forms in the Kingdoms of Nature

Space is the field in which these energies and forces of constellations, solar systems, and planets play and function. When passing through our planet Earth, they produce effects upon it as a whole and upon us individually. To understand and learn about the sources of these conditioning and governing energies and forces and their relationships between individuals, planetary, systemic, and cosmic entities will expand our horizon, and we shall begin to live scientifically. We are part of a greater whole and can become consciously aware of it. Space is an entity, and the entire "vault of heaven" is its phenomenal appearance. Humanity as a whole is

19

an entity, expressing itself through the many diversified forms of human beings; yet each is a part of the phenomenal entity we call humanity.[2]

NOTES

1. *Esoteric Astrology*, pp. 5–15.
2. Ibid., pp. 24, 556, 606–9.

VII. *Our Solar Life or Logos* is on the second cosmic ray of love-wisdom. The seven rays that function within our solar system are seven sub-rays of the second cosmic ray. Although functioning to a lesser degree as their cosmic prototypes, all are tinged with the powers of love-wisdom. Their function is to develop consciousness.

In this illustration of our solar system the Sun is not shown in proper proportion to the planets. In proportion to our Earth, which is shown as

VII   The Cosmic Ray of
Our Solar System

In our present solar system only one of the Seven Cosmic Rays is in operation. *Our Solar Life*, or *Solar Logos*, is on the second *Cosmic Ray of Love-Wisdom.*

The Seven Rays that function within our solar system are seven sub-rays of the second Cosmic Ray. Therefore, while functioning to a lesser degree as their cosmic prototype, all seven are always tinged with the powers of Love-Wisdom. Each one of these seven sub-rays is an expression of a Solar Life and is the recipient and custodian of energies coming from seven solar systems and twelve constellations. These Seven Rays embody seven types of force that demonstrate to us the seven qualities of the ONE.

The seven differentiations of one great cosmic ray were effected within the very being of our Solar Logos before He began His creation. Therefore we know that the divine spark, the divine centre of consciousness within each one of us, comes from the highest principle of our Solar Logos and has within it the potentiality of all the Rays. Each one is colored primarily by the special attributes of one or another of the Cosmic Rays because each sub-ray is, in essence and effect, the same as the Greater Cosmic Ray.

¼" in diameter, the Sun should be between 25" and 26" in diameter. We can then readily see how only a very small amount of solar radiation hits our Earth; but that seems to be just the right amount of light, warmth, love, and (it is to be hoped) wisdom to let us and all on earth live and grow.

The differentiation into seven sub-rays took place within our Solar Logos before He started His creation. And all seven sub-rays have, in addition to the emphasis of the Primary Ray, the same characteristics, qualities, and purpose as the Seven Cosmic Rays.

The purpose of our solar system is to unfold consciousness. The goal of the evolutionary process in humanity is the achievement of full awareness of the nature of forms and the nature of their ensouling entities, which will effect in human beings an expansion from self-consciousness to group-consciousness to God-consciousness.[1]

NOTES

1. *Esoteric Psychology* I, pp. 168–69.

VIII. *Seven Stars of the Great Bear Are the Originating Source of the Seven Rays of Our Solar System.* Each ray transmits its energies through three constellations of the zodiac to our sun which then reach our earth primarily through one of the sacred planets.

VIII   The Seven Rays of
Our Solar System

By analogy to the cosmic Trinity, we see our Solar Logos as a Trinity of Spirit, Consciousness, and Matter, or as D. K. often speaks of it, as Life, Quality, and Appearance. The Rays that function in our solar system as the seven sub-rays of the second Cosmic Ray of Love-Wisdom originate in seven stars of the Great Bear. In this illustration we see the three stars on top, representing the Rays of Aspect, and below these three the four Rays of Attribute. These seven ray energies reach our Sun by way of the twelve constellations of the Zodiac. Each Ray transmits its energy through three constellations and reaches our earth primarily through one of the seven sacred planets.

RAY	CONSTELLATIONS	PLANETS
1. Will or Power	♈ ♌ ♑ Aries Leo Capricorn	Vulcan V
2. Love-Wisdom	♊ ♍ ♓ Gemini Virgo Pisces	Jupiter ♃
3. Active Intelligence	♋ ♎ ♑ Cancer Libra Capricorn	Saturn ♄
4. Harmony through Conflict	♉ ♏ ♐ Taurus Scorpio Sagittarius	Mercury ☿
5. Concrete Science	♌ ♐ ♒ Leo Sagittarius Aquarius	Venus ♀

27

6. *Idealism,*   ♍   ♐   ♓
   Devotion   *Virgo Sagittarius Pisces*   *Neptune* ♆

7. *Ceremonial*   ♈   ♋   ♑
   Order   *Aries Cancer Capricorn*   *Uranus* ♅

See *Esoteric Astrology*, pp. 86, 423, 513, 590,649.

At present and for millions of years, our solar system revolves in the heavens within the circle of what we call the greater Zodiac—a 25,000-year cycle—and in a lesser cycle during the course of the twelve months of the year. Because every planet is linked with the Sun and every other planet, the interplay and interrelation of influences of these Ray-Lives have effects upon our planetary Life as a whole and upon each individual human being and every living thing on earth.

Our solar system is a vast intelligent organism with many planetary centers—sacred and non-sacred—that are the conscious instruments through which the universal drama is enacted, just as by analogy on human scale the organs within our own makeup enable us to manifest, to think, to feel, and to act.

These seven potent ray energies produce on our as-yet non-sacred planet Earth what is called *transformations*, which bring individual human beings increasingly in line with the will of Divinity. Because the influences of the Rays are mostly concerned with the stimulation of the soul, they bring about changes in consciousness.

The individual human being becomes gradually fitted to respond to the soul and to unfold his latent possibilities. With increasing response to these energies the evolutionary process is hastened, the unfoldment of the inner life takes place, and the soul begins consciously to travel back to his source. Nothing and no one can escape the radiatory and magnetic influences of the Rays. Each person is sensitive, and responds, to Ray stimulations according to the point of achievement reached on the path of evolution or according to the extent of soul contact and adherence to the higher values of life.

In this tremendous interplay of energies and forces, the wonder of it all is the fact that insistent signs of Order, Beauty, and Rhythm can everywhere be found and that nothing can prevent the eventual manifestation of the Glory of God.[1]

Ray I, the Lord of Will or Power, expresses Himself in our solar system primarily through the planet *Vulcan* (hidden by the Sun). He is a Life that wills to love and that uses power as an expression of His divine beneficence. In the unfolding plan of the Logos, *will* demonstrates as power. The energies of Ray I come through *Aries, Leo,* and *Capricorn.* Of this triangle *Aries* is today the controlling factor and is the source of the initial energy producing the New Age.[2]

The motto of Ray I is: "I hold the key of life and death; I bind and loose again; I the destroyer am." His word is power, His light is electric, the lightning is His symbol. His robe of blue veils His eternal purpose, but in the rising and the setting sun His orb of red is seen.

The sense of touch is related in a peculiar way to the first Ray of Will or Power as the "Finger of God" (which brings to mind Michelangelo's picture of Creation on the ceiling of the Sistine Chapel in Rome). D. K. says, "Through the application of the Finger of God in its directing and forceful work, we have the cyclic destruction of forms, so that the manifestation of Deity may grow in power and beauty. Thus the Lord of Power or Will performs the task of destruction, thereby bringing beauty into being and the revelation of God's will and his beneficent purpose." This destruction can be witnessed today in every field of endeavour as old forms are broken down so that new and better ones can be built.

There is no true Ray I type in incarnation as yet. Ray I will come into full play only when the time comes for the divine purpose to be safely revealed. All so-called Ray I egos are on the first sub-ray of the second Cosmic Ray, which is in incarnation.

Viewed symbolically, Ray I embodies the dynamic idea of God, and thus the Most High starts the work of creation.[3]

Ray II, the Lord of Love-Wisdom, is, in our solar system, the expression of the Cosmic Christ. He is the embodiment of pure love who instills into all forms the quality of love and is in our solar system the most potent of the Seven Rays. He expresses Himself primarily through the planet *Jupiter*, which is His body of manifestation. Originating in a star of the Great Bear, this Ray-Life transmits its energies to our solar system through the constellations of *Gemini, Virgo,* and *Pisces.* At this time the controlling factor is *Virgo*, which produces the increased activity of the Christ principle in the hearts of humanity.[2]

In these two rays of *Will* and *Love* we have the two main characteristics of the divine nature that lie latent behind all the myriads of forms. Human beings are the custodians of that wisdom which will enable them to further the divine Plan and bring it to fruition. That certainly puts a great responsibility upon each one of us and humanity as a whole, but we also have the honour and privilege of being co-workers with our Logos in objectifying His plan of creation.

Ray II is the Ray of the Master Builder who is occupied with the first formulation of the plan upon which the forms must be constructed and the idea of the Most High materialised. Through Him the blueprints come into being with their mathematical accuracy, their structural unity, and their geometrical perfection, which then makes the work of the actual builders possible.

Specific qualities that Ray II represents are: love divine, radiance, attraction, the power to save, wisdom, expansion, and inclusiveness. The mystery of Ray II is found hidden in the significance of the perfume of flowers. Ray II is one of the three Rays that are responsible for the development of consciousness in the vegetable kingdom, whose highest development is attractiveness, magnetism, and perfume.[4]

Ray III, the Ray of Active Intelligence, is the expression of the third person of the Trinity, the Holy Ghost. On cosmic levels it is the inherent intelligence in matter. The Lord of Ray III is responsible for the actual working out of the Plan and bringing into objectivity the divine creation of the entire visible worlds, using the mind and all means needed to materialise the divine idea. According to D. K., this third ray activity of impregnating matter with intelligence was dominant in our solar system during the first manifestation of our Solar Logos. He is now in His second phase of manifestation on the second major Ray of Love-Wisdom, and in His next manifestation the first Ray of Will and Power will be dominant.

The third Ray of Aspect is called the Ray of Active Intelligence because its work is more closely linked with matter. It is also the personality Ray of our planetary Logos. And since we live within the periphery of our planetary Logos, all of humanity is strongly influenced by this third ray energy of active intelligence. It is, in fact, the personality aspect in every human being that the Soul created and uses to experience and express its essential divinity. It is under the influence of Ray III that we learn to create until we become co-creators with Divinity Itself. This Ray-Lord works in close cooperation with the Lord of the second Ray because He constitutes the active building force that starts the work of construction and eventually materialises the idea and purpose of God. Yet these three Rays of Will, Love-Wisdom, and Active Intelligence are as much a unity as is a human being who conceives an idea, uses his mind and brain to bring the idea into manifestation, and employs hands and all his natural forces to perfect the idea.[5]

These three major Rays correspond in the human being to the Monad, Soul, and Personality. The third ray energy, coming from the Great Bear, reaches our sun through the zodiacal triangle of *Cancer, Libra,* and *Capricorn.* Its body of expression is primarily the planet *Saturn.* Together they provide humanity, through the medium of matter, with a vast field of experiment and experience. At this time *Cancer* is the controlling factor as its energy causes the mass movement towards liberty, release, and light that is so dominant today.[2]

Summarizing the three major Rays of Aspect, we could say: Life is One, and God is One; but for a more intelligent understanding of the divine qualities and purpose, D. K. speaks of three Rays of Aspect and four Rays of Attribute. *Ray I*, the reflection of the Father aspect, is the *Ray of Will or Power*, the Monad, the Spirit, the One who conceives the original plan of creation. *Ray II of Love-Wisdom* is the Son aspect of the Trinity, the Soul or consciousness, the Master Builder who works out the blueprints for creation. *Ray III of Active Intelligence* connotes the actual builders and materialisers of the divine plan of creation, the workers who bring the master Plan into objectivity. This scheme of creation applies, whether we speak of creation on cosmic, solar, planetary, or human levels, for each is a Trinity within the outer form.

The Four Rays of Attribute

In our solar system, and especially on our planet Earth, the four Rays of Attribute express in greater detail the qualities, characteristics, and purpose of the three major Rays. They widen the scope of the Rays of Aspect and are synthesised in the third major Ray of Active Intelligence. They are:

Ray IV, The Ray of Harmony through Conflict

Ray V, The Ray of Concrete Knowledge and Science

Ray VI, The Ray of Idealism and Devotion

Ray VII, The Ray of Ceremonial Magic and Order

Ray IV, the Ray of Harmony, Beauty, and Art, has for its function the creation of beauty through the free interplay of life and form, basing its design of beauty upon the initial Plan as it exists in the mind of our Solar Logos. Its keynote is harmony through conflict, harmony between the desires of the form (or personality) and the desires of the indwelling life. Its purpose is to produce at-one-ment, unity, beauty, and balance. This makes the fourth ray energy essentially a force for wholeness and healing as it helps all forms to achieve an ultimate perfection through the power of the inner life.

This fourth Ray of Beauty, Harmony, and Art gives to all forms that which produces beauty and works towards the harmonising of all effects emanating from the world of causes; it is the producer of the quality of organisation through form. It is the Ray of mathematical exactitude and *not* the Ray of the artist, because artistic endeavour plays an essential role in every field of activity.

Ray IV is essentially the refiner, the producer of perfection within the form, and the prime manipulator of the energies of God. It works in such a way that the Temple of the Lord is indeed known in its true nature as that which "houses" the Light. It is primarily expressive on the plane of intuition and is the way of the seeker, the searcher, the sensitive reflector of beauty.

Like the three major Rays of Aspect, each of the four Rays of Attribute has its origin in one of the seven stars of the Great Bear. Fourth ray energy comes through *Taurus, Scorpio,* and *Sagittarius*, of which *Scorpio* is today the controlling factor. Through Scorpio comes the testing of humanity as the world disciple.[2] Mercury is the sacred planet through which the Lord of the fourth Ray expresses Himself primarily.

Because humanity is the fourth kingdom of nature, existing between the three lower kingdoms—animal, vegetable, mineral—and the three higher kingdoms—that of the Soul, the Monad, and Divinity—it stands at a point of balance between opposites, between the world of the personality and the world of the soul, between objective and subjective forces, between illusion and reality. This balance and harmony that the fourth ray energy promotes and produces is beautifully stated by D. K. in the following mantram:

> Color and yet no color now is seen.
> Sound and the soundless One meet in an infinite point of peace.
> Time and the timeless One negate the thoughts of men . . .

Form is there found, and yet the psychic sense reveals that
which the form is powerless to hide—the inner
synthesis . . .
Form and its soul are merged.
The inner vision watches over the fusion, knows the divine
relation and sees the two as one. But from that point of
high attainment a higher vision blazes forth before the
opened inner eye . . .
Pass on, O Pilgrim on the Way.[6]

Ray V, the Ray of Concrete Knowledge and Science, is the stream
of energy behind which stands the Lord of Knowledge and Science. This great Life is in close touch with the mind of the
Creator. It is the Ray of Science and of Research. In both fields of
endeavour much attention has been given to the outer forms of
life, but now a beam of light illuminates the form, the hidden
knowledge of God and how He veils Himself, and finds its way
into human minds and thoughts. Energies and forces reveal their
inner purpose, and much is seen as process, as rhythm, and as
returning on itself. This is exactly what subatomic research and
biochemistry are bringing out through scientists like Fritjof
Capra, author of *The Tao of Physics*; the biochemist Albert
Szent-Györgyi; Gary Zukav; and others.

The purpose of the form is to reveal the mind and the love of
God. The past reveals the form, but the present indicates the flow-
ing in of energy. In connection with Ray V, we find in a sort of
mystical mantram by the Tibetan Master these words: "That
which is on its way comes as a cloud which veils the sun. But hid
behind this cloud of immanence is love, and on the earth is love
and in the heaven is love, and this—the love which maketh all
things new—must stand revealed. This is the purpose back of all
the acts of this great Lord of Knowledge and of Science, the Lord
of the fifth Ray."[7]

This fifth ray energy is one of unique and peculiar potency in
relation to humanity because the plane of mind is the sphere of its
major activity. It also has much to do with the transfer of the

human consciousness into the fifth or spiritual kingdom. Just as the personality has no other function in the divine Plan than to be the medium of expression of the soul, so is the lower mind intended to be a channel for the inflow of higher mind energy. Under the influence of this fifth Ray, love and mind must eventually and naturally reveal each other.

Fifth ray energy comes to our solar system by way of *Leo, Sagittarius,* and *Aquarius* and expresses itself primarily through the planet *Venus.* Leo is the controlling factor at this time because Leo produces the growth of individualism and of self-consciousness that is today so prevalent on a world scale.[2]

Our present Aryan race, the fifth root-race, is strongly influenced by the fifth ray energy with its keynote of mental development. This may account for our strong emphasis today on education, science, technology, and psychology. The mental plane, however, is a dual plane of lower concrete mind and higher mind. Through the energy of Ray V we learn to know our world of forms, not only for their own sake but as prerequisites to the higher and deeper understanding of their true purpose that sees the outer forms as instruments to soul purpose and quality. "The higher mind must be allowed to purify the lower mind in order to make it the powerful and constructive tool it is meant to be. . . . When the knowledge of God shall shine forth universally . . . the expression through the human instrumentality of the divine omniscience, then will the Lord of Concrete Science, Who is the embodiment of the fifth principle of mind, see His work brought to a conclusion."[7]

Ray VI, the Ray of Devotion and Idealism, is the stream of divine energy that is transmitted to our solar system by way of *Virgo, Sagittarius,* and *Pisces.* The energies of this triangle of constellations pour at present into our solar and planetary life especially through *Sagittarius* as this sign produces the focussed, one-pointed effort of the world aspirant.[2] Its planetary expression is primarily the sacred planet *Neptune.* This ray force of idealism and devotion, together with the second Ray of Love-Wisdom, is considered a true and vital expression of the divine nature. "A militant focussing upon the ideal, a one-pointed devotion to the intent of the life urge, and a divine sincerity are the qualities of this Lord, and they set their impress upon all that is found within His body of manifestation."[8] There is a certain mystical relationship between Ray II, Ray IV, and Ray VI. Ray VI is the reflection of Ray II, and Ray IV of Harmony through Conflict brings about through suffering and pain the transmutation of love and devotion on lower levels to the purified, unselfish, and inclusive love and devotion on soul levels. Within the sixth ray energy are the powers that help us to transmute glamour, which is so prominent on the astral plane, into the clear light of the intuition, when the mind has purified the emotions. Under sixth ray influences we learn to transform our selfish and personal motivations for service to the unselfish, impersonal devotion and service to higher values and for the good of all.

During the past 2000 years the sixth ray influences have strongly coloured our civilisation and religious life, but its power is now passing out of manifestation to be replaced by the seventh ray of Ceremonial Magic and Order, for which the activities of Ray VI have laid the foundation. Old crystallised forms disappear, which gives the new order of the seventh Ray a chance to synthesise and manifest the good which the Piscean Age has produced. This may be responsible for the many New Age and esoteric groups springing up, and for the literature on meditation—Eastern and Western —which is flooding the market today.

The Master D. K. himself has made the effort to teach the new psychology to show us what our equipment is, and how well it is suited to the work for which we have been created. We know that during the past hundred years the world has been changed beyond belief; and we can assume that the coming changes will be still more rapid and deep-seated, for the growth of intellectual powers is gathering momentum, and according to D. K., man the creator is coming into possession of his powers. When the "Desire of all Nations," the Cosmic Christ, shall stand revealed, all human beings and all creatures shall occultly "taste" or share in that great happening. And the Lord of the sixth Ray of Devotion and Idealism shall see the consummation of His work and be satisfied.[8]

Ray VII, the Ray of Ceremonial Magic and Order, embodies the quality or principle that coordinates and unifies the inner quality and the outer tangible form or appearance. This is its true magical work through Law and Order. This Lord of Law and Order, whose powerful energy is now coming in and making its pressure felt, has a peculiar power on our physical plane, for there is a close numerical interrelation between the seventh Ray and the seventh plane, which is the physical, just as the seventh root-race will see complete conformity to, and a perfect expression of, Law and Order. We are now in the fifth root-race, approaching the sixth; and in the seventh we shall see the fruition of our efforts of today.

As the *reflection* of the first ray of *Will and Power*, the power of *the seventh Ray* is inherent in physical matter. We need only to think of the power stored in the very atom, in mountains, volcanoes, hurricanes, and earthquakes. However, according to D. K., these forces of nature can and will ultimately be geared toward a higher purpose and used constructively and harmlessly.

The first powerful effects of the seventh ray energies are changes along the line of destroying crystallised forms in order to release the true values hidden in the forms, which are law and order and peaceful coexistence. Through the Lord of the seventh Ray, the will aspect of Divinity becomes expressed and focused on earth as He brings into objective manifestation—by an act of will—both spirit and matter, with the help of the third Ray of Active intelligence, which expresses itself through humanity and its individual members.[9]

Here, too, we can sense the purpose of this great Lord of Ray VII in excerpts of a mantram that D. K. gave us to ponder: "Let the Temple of the Lord be built. . . . Seven great sons of God . . . took their seats. The work of building thus began. . . . The light shone dim. . . . The seven were silent and their forms were veiled. . . . between the seven Forms the work went on. . . . The door was opened and the door was shut. Each time it opened, the power within the temple grew; each time the light waxed stronger, for one by one the sons of men entered the temple. . . . Its lines, its walls, its decorations . . . emerged. . . . The Word went forth: Open the door to all the sons of men who come . . . and seek the temple of the Lord. Give them the light. . . . Sound forth the Word creative and raise the dead to life. . . . the craftsmen are prepared. God has created in the light. His sons can now create. . . . "Let the work proceed. Let the sons of God create."[10]

To create the Temple of the Lord, through building the right thought-forms, seems to be our responsibility now. D. K. points out that the need is great for a sound teaching concerning the laws of thought and the rules that govern the building of those thought-forms that must embody the ideas that emanate from the universal Mind. We must begin on the subjective planes of life to work out the needed order. Then, when that is realized, we shall have every important group of people engaged in world affairs and aided by trained thinkers, so that the right application and correct adjustment to the plan will eventuate. In *A Treatise on White Magic* we can learn all about building the right thought-forms. One by one we undergo the esoteric and spiritual counter-part of what is called "a mental test." That test will demonstrate a person's usefulness in mental work and power and will show the capacity to build thought-forms, to vitalise them, and so to enter the temple as a creative worker, aiding the magical work of the Temple Guardian, the Lord of the seventh Ray.

In our solar system, the energies of the seventh Ray are transmitted by way of *Aries, Cancer,* and *Capricorn,* reaching our Earth primarily through the sacred planet *Uranus.* Of this triangle of zodiacal signs, Capricorn is today the controlling factor, as the Capricornian energy produces the overcoming of materialism and leads to the mountaintop, to initiation.[2]

This Ray Lord builds through the power of thought; and so are we at lower levels building a new civilisation through our thinking and objectifying our ideas in outer manifestation.

The sense of hearing corresponds in a peculiar way to the seventh Ray. "Through the Words of Power the worlds came into ordered being and the Lord of the Ray of Ceremonial Magic brings about the organisation of this divine organism." *This is the Ray that makes a human being delight in "all things done decently and in order and according to rule and precedent."* The main work of the seventh Ray might be seen in the spiritualising of the forms, and it is this principle of fusion, of coordination and blending, that is active every time a soul comes into incarnation and a child is born on earth.[10]

Now that we have glimpsed a little of the functioning of these most powerful streams of divine energy on cosmic, solar, planetary and human levels, *what do they really mean to us*? The Tibetan Master gives us the answer: "The goal of evolution for humanity is to become consciously and livingly aware of the nature of these energies and begin to know and use them. . . . Even a dim perception of that vast aggregation of intelligent Forces . . . will serve to bring into clearer light the realisation that our solar system" and consequently our earth and we ourselves are part of this immense interrelation of energies and forces. "Because these forces are, we are; because They persist, we persist; because They move in form and space and time, we do the same."[11]

NOTES

1. See *Esoteric Astrology*, pp. 602–12.
2. *Esoteric Astrology*, p. 490.
3. See *Esoteric Psychology* I for Ray I, pp. 27, 46, 63, 133, 159–63.
4. See Ibid. for Ray II, pp. 46–159.
5. See Ibid. for Ray III, pp. 159–63.
6. See Ibid. for Ray IV, pp. 70–71.
7. See Ibid. for Ray V, pp. 74–77, 134.
8. See Ibid. for Ray VI, pp. 25, 81–83, 133–34.
9. *Esoteric Astrology*, pp. 138–39.
10. See *Esoteric Psychology* I for Ray VII, pp. 83–85, 133, 210.
11. *Esoteric Astrology*, pp. 23, 607–9.

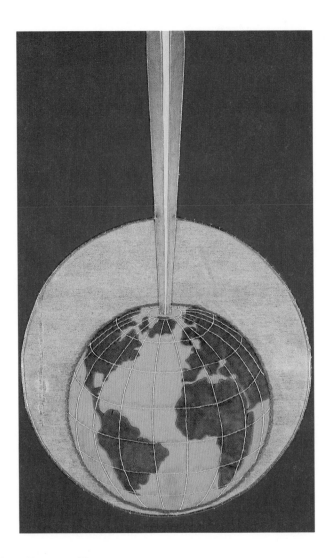

IX. *OUR PLANET EARTH* IS THE EMBODIMENT OF A GREAT LIVING CONSCIOUS ENTITY WHO WORKS THROUGH A PLANETARY CENTER OR GROUP CONSISTING OF THE LORD OF THE WORLD AND HIS COUNCIL. THE PERSONALITY RAY OF THIS GREAT BEING IS THE THIRD RAY OF ACTIVE INTELLIGENCE, WHICH AT THIS TIME DOMINATES HUMANITY.

IX OUR WORLD

The *World* we see is but the outer form, the personality aspect, of a much greater invisible living Entity, our *planetary Logos*. This great Being is primarily conditioned by a Cosmic Ray. His *personality Ray*, not His soul Ray, is the *Ray of Active Intelligence*, which at this time dominates humanity. We have therefore a humanity engrossed by a tremendous activity, demonstrating everywhere a vital discriminating and intellectual interest in all types of phenomena. Humanity is with great speed integrating the three aspects of human nature—physical, emotional, mental—into one expression, the personality, and is therefore more able to respond to the Ray of the integrated personality of the ONE in Whom we live and move and have our being.

Our planetary Logos, whose consciousness reaches into solar and cosmic realms, causes the evolution of consciousness within all kingdoms of nature and leads humanity through the powers and influences of the cyclically manifesting Seven Rays from self-centeredness to ever greater inclusiveness and finally to Soul- and God-consciousness. The goal of every conscious life below the human is self-consciousness; the goal of every human and superhuman being is God-consciousness.

Each of the seven sub-rays of the second cosmic Ray of Love-Wisdom, the Ray of our Sun, embodies the energy, will, love, and purpose of the Lord of our solar system, but each ray also has its specific qualities to transmit. "It is the quality of a Ray-Life in time and space which determines the phenomenal appearance." And quality is the second manifesting aspect of Divinity, the quality that emerges under the impulse of divine life as love, with the aim of ultimate synthesis in consciousness.

The objective of our present evolutionary process is the unfoldment of conscious awareness, and quality is the nature of that awareness. This leads to an understanding of the response of an individual consciousness to the consciousness contacted. There

41

are energies that lie behind the outer appearances. It is this interplay between the consciousnesses that gives an understanding of quality, of the activity and the motivation underlying the appearance. These energies we seek to bring out and understand as we sense the beauties that lie unrevealed behind all forms.[1]

Among the planets in our solar system that are interrelated and interdependent, our Earth stands for the sphere of experience. The line of least resistance is, for humanity, harmony through conflict.[2]

NOTES

1. *Esoteric Psychology* I, pp. 191–95, 335–42.
2. *Esoteric Astrology*, pp. 126–27.

X. *Under the Influence of the Seven Rays, Each Kingdom in Nature Develops One Outstanding Quality in its Consciousness.*

In the mineral kingdom it is the quality of radioactivity.
In the vegetable kingdom it is the quality of attractiveness through colour and perfume.
In the animal kingdom it is the quality of domesticity and devotion to human beings.
In the human kingdom the emerging quality is intuition—recognition of divine realities.

X   The Rays and the Four Kingdoms of Nature

Under the influences of the Seven Rays, each kingdom in nature has developed or is developing one outstanding quality.

In the *mineral kingdom* it is the quality of activity with its two extremes of the static, inert nature and the quality of radioactivity or radiation, which is its beautiful and divinely perfected expression. This radioactivity is the goal for all mineral atomic forms.

The *vegetable kingdom* has the quality of attractiveness expressed in colour; its highest activity is the perfume of its highest forms of life.

The *animal kingdom* has the quality of unfolding instinctual purpose, which in its highest form works out as domesticity and devotion to human beings. Behind the appearances of the animals is a steady orientation towards understanding, which comes through the influence of the Fifth Ray of Concrete Knowledge, pouring through the human family upon the third kingdom of nature. Man is to lead the animal kingdom towards liberation—a liberation into the fourth kingdom, which is the sphere of its next activity. The problem of pain, bloodshed, war, and suffering will be solved only when man himself has changed the initiating process for animals and his own animal body to that of domesticity and mutual love.

The emerging quality in the *human kingdom* is intuition. Man harmonizes in himself all ways of release and all achievements; he synthesises in his life the aspirations of the other three kingdoms. A human being is also intended to be radioactive, and the perfume of his life must ascend and attract the forces that lead him to his liberation. The unfolding purpose of his animal form must give place to the dynamic will of the spiritual entity in order for the divine qualities to emerge and appear in their full glory. Man develops and unfolds within himself the needed apparatus of response by training himself to recognise the subjective realities or the *divine qualities* as they seek to manifest.[1]

NOTES

1. See *Esoteric Psychology* I, pp. 191–200, 319–28.

XI. In the *Mineral Kingdom*, the seventh ray of organisation and the first ray of power are the dominant factors affecting the development of consciousness within the mineral forms. This process leads from the static mineral stage through that of crystal, semiprecious, and precious stone to that of radioactive substance.

XI   Rays and the Mineral Kingdom

Certain Rays are more responsible than others for the qualifying of any particular kingdom, although in the entire process of perfection all kingdoms are cyclically under the influence of all Seven Rays.

In the mineral kingdom, the *seventh Ray of Organisation* and the *first Ray of Power* are the dominant factors affecting the quality and consciousness of the mineral forms. The three stages of the evolutionary process within the life cycle of every mineral lead from the static mineral stage, such as carbon, through that of crystal, semiprecious stones, and precious stones to that of the radioactive substances. These developments are greatly enhanced whenever the seventh Ray comes in, as is the case now and shall be for the next 2000 years.

The seventh Ray is one of Organized Ritual, which, in the building of forms, is a basic and necessary quality. The first ray influence is indicated in the fact that the processes found in the mineral kingdom are profoundly geometrical. Symbolically speaking, the mineral kingdom marks the point of unique condensation of precipitated etheric substance, brought about under the action of fire and by the pressure of the "divine idea." This condensation is the tangible result of the interplay of the energies and qualities of the first and seventh Rays.

"The divine plan is hidden in the geometry of a crystal; and God's radiant beauty is stored in the color of a precious stone." If "matter is spirit at the lowest point of its cyclic activity" and spirit is matter at its highest, then the Ray of Ceremonial Order is but the polar opposite of the First Ray of Will or Power. The geometrical faculty of the Universal Mind finds its most material perfection on the physical plane, working through the seventh Ray. The result of this interplay is an eventual transmutation of the Earth's substance to radioactivity and radiation.

The mineral kingdom holds in solution all the forces and those chemicals and minerals that are needed by the forms in other kingdoms. It constitutes the "foundation" of the ordered physical structure of our planet. The Earth and its molten content are the united production of the Will of the first Ray and the Ordered Rhythm of the seventh Ray.

Through the agencies of fire, intense heat, and pressure, a division of the mineral kingdom into three parts has already occurred: the baser metals, the standard metals (gold, silver), and the semi-precious stones and crystals. The precious jewels are a synthesis of all three and mark one of the basic syntheses of evolution.

In order to understand the rays and their bearing on life as a whole, it is necessary that we grasp the fact that man is only a small fraction of the whole, that he has his roots in all three kingdoms, and that all have contributed to his equipment. He unites the three lower kingdoms to the three higher. The sign of man's spiritual unfoldment lies in his ability to include in his consciousness not only the so-called spiritual values and the power to reach soul contact, but also the material values and the power divinely to reach the potencies that lie hidden from him in the custody of the other forms of life found in the three subhuman kingdoms.[1]

When the proper and correct Ray stimulation is applied to the *soul in any form*, then the soul will do its own work of destruction, of attraction, of rebuilding, and of a consequently renewed life manifestation. This is also true of the soul of a human being, of a nation, and of humanity itself. It is for this reason that the seventh Ray is governing the mineral kingdom and manifesting through it that significant soul quality of radiation. This word *radiation* describes the result of soul stimulation upon and within every form, as the life of the soul eventually radiates beyond the form and produces definite effects.[2]

NOTES

1. See *Esoteric Psychology* I, pp. 223–31.
2. *Destiny of the Nations*, p. 123.

XII. IN THE *VEGETABLE KINGDOM* THE INFLUENCES OF THREE RAYS ARE BLENDED AND FUSED: RAY II OF LOVE-WISDOM, RAY IV OF HARMONY THROUGH CONFLICT, AND RAY VI OF DEVOTION AND IDEALISM. THESE PRODUCE A FOURFOLD PERFECTION: MAGNETISM, COLOUR AND COLOUR HARMONY, PERFUME, AND GROWTH TOWARD THE LIGHT. ALL THESE BLEND IN MAGNETIC RADIATION—MINERAL AND VEGETABLE GOALS COMBINED.

XII   Rays and the Vegetable Kingdom

The vegetable kingdom is the only subhuman kingdom of nature in which the influences of three Rays are blended and fused. Their combined activity has produced a fourfold perfection in this kingdom: the perfection of *magnetism,* of *colour* and *colour harmony,* of *perfume,* and of *growth towards the light.* The Rays responsible for this perfection are Ray II, Ray IV, and Ray VI.

The **second Ray of Love-Wisdom** is working out as a vastly increased sensibility. The result of these second ray influences, which pour cyclically through this kingdom, has been to produce its magnetism and its attractiveness. Some of its beneficent influence expresses itself through the cereals and flowers.

The **fourth Ray of Harmony through Conflict** is working out in the harmonisation of plant life throughout the entire planet. Its object is the production of harmony between form and life. It brings about the beautiful harmony of colour in nature and produces a synthesis and uniformity in the greens, the grasses, and the smaller forms of vegetable life that cover our whole planet.

The **sixth Ray of Devotion and Idealism** effects growth towards the light, the "urge to consecrate the life to the sun, the giver of that life." This Ray determines the type, family, appearance, strength, and size of the trees upon the planet. It influences the normal tendency of all life-forms to evolve. It has brought to the surface the seeds of the vegetable kingdom latent within the soil. It is through the growth towards an ideal or a divine prototype that this Ray of devotion brings about the urge to evolve.

The united effort of these three Rays has brought forth the perfume of the flowers as found in the higher units of the vegetable kingdom. All these results of magnetism, colour, perfume, and

53

growth towards the light blend in *magnetic radiation*—the mineral and vegetable goals combined.

The evolution of consciousness that started in the mineral world reaches, in the vegetable kingdom, a greater state of perfection, because it adds to the brilliance in the mineral kingdom the magnetism, colour, perfume, and the trend towards the light. "It is in this kingdom that one first sees clearly the glory which lies ahead of humanity." Because of three basic Ray influences, the vegetable kingdom is more evolved along its own peculiar lines than any other kingdom in nature. The planets Venus and Jupiter powerfully influence this world of vegetable forms.

The Rays that actually influence nature at any time establish a relation between the kingdoms, increase the interplay and interchange of energies and forces, and thus produce new effects, new forms of life, and new wonders in the world of phenomena.

The vegetable kingdom with its trees and shrubs, its flowering plants, its green things and grasses all over the world is the outstanding contribution of our planet Earth to the general Solar Plan.[1]

NOTES

1. See *Esoteric Psychology* I, pp. 233-51.

XIII. *The Development of Consciousness in the Animal Kingdom* is influenced first by the third ray of active intelligence, producing a certain one-pointedness, and then by the sixth ray of devotion, which produces a relation to human beings. Its outstanding achievements are intelligence and devotion. The early blending of psychological factors leads finally to the process of individualisation.

XIII   Rays and the Animal Kingdom

In the animal kingdom the influence of the *third Ray of Active Intelligence*, or Adaptability, is potent and will increase until it has produced in the animal world a reaction to life that can be described as "animal one-pointedness." Then at this point and cyclically, the *Sixth Ray of Devotion and Idealism* can make its pressure felt as the urge towards a goal and produce a relation to man. This can be seen in the tamed, trained, and domesticated animals. The third Ray of Active Intelligence produces the emergence of instinct, which in turn creates and uses that marvellous response apparatus we call the nervous system, the brain, and the five senses. There is a much closer relation existing between the animal and man than between the animal and the vegetable.

In the animal kingdom the first dim indications of sorrow and pain are seen. These educating processes are more indicated in the domesticated animals. The animal suffers, but suffers entirely physically and sentiently, while human beings also suffer mentally. Under the influence of the sixth Ray appears the power to be domesticated and trained, which finally leads to the power to love, to serve, and to emerge from the herd into the group. For the first time we have in this kingdom an authentic organisation of the "true nerves and sensory centers." Both the animal and the human being share the general grouping of nerves and force centers, a spinal column, and a brain. We have in the animal the early blending of psychological factors—a process of life-giving, of intelligent integration, and of psychological unfoldment to meet emergencies, which finally lead to the process of individualisation.

The animal kingdom is divided into three categories: first, the higher and domesticated animals such as the dog, cat, horse, and elephant; second, the so-called wild animals such as the lion, tiger, and other wild animals; third, the mass of lesser animals such as rodents.

The purpose of the animal world is called *experimentation*, which connotes a great mystery peculiar to our planet. The objective of the experimentation might be stated as follows: "It is the intent of the planetary Logos to bring about a psychological condition . . . of 'divine lucidity.' The work of the psyche and the goal of the true psychology, is to see life clearly, as it is, and with all that is involved. This does not mean conditions and environment, but Life. This process was begun in the animal kingdom, and will be consummated in the human."

Two major Rays are functioning in both the animal world and the human world. However, the third Ray of Active Intelligence functions more potently and influences more powerfully in the animal kingdom than in man. In the animal kingdom as a whole, the third and sixth Rays are predominant, but each animal is also subject to its own Ray impulses. For instance: dogs are expressions of the second Ray, cats of the third Ray, and horses of the sixth Ray.

Man's work for the animal world is to transmit divine energy to a waiting world of forms and to stimulate instinct until individualisation is possible. The planetary influences that play more specifically upon the animal kingdom are those of the Moon and Mars, thereby bringing about desired results in the third kingdom of nature.

Human responsibility in relation to animals lies along the line of the two divine aspects that are already embodied in the animal world. They are the third Ray of Active Intelligence and the second Ray of Love. The latter is present in the animal as herd instinct. The animal's love and attention should under human influence be turned increasingly towards its master. It is through the power of thought that man will eventually bridge the gap existing between the animal and man—controlled and directed thought that controls and directs the consciousness of the animal.[1]

NOTES

1. See *Esoteric Psychology* I, pp. 251-58.

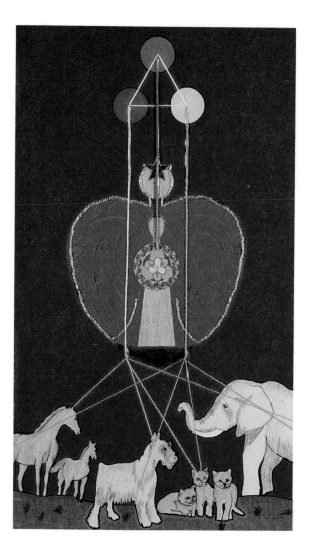

XIV. *INDIVIDUALISATION* IS THE TRANSITION FROM ANIMAL CON-
SCIOUSNESS TO SELF-CONSCIOUSNESS IN THE HUMAN BEING WHEN ALL
THREE DIVINE ASPECTS APPEAR IN A UNIT OF LIFE IN FORM. TO THE
TWO ALREADY FUNCTIONING ASPECTS OF ACTIVE INTELLIGENCE (RAY
III) AND LOVE (RAY II) IS ADDED RAY I OF WILL AND POWER. THIS
HIGHER ASPECT TAKES THE INITIATIVE AND, THROUGH A STIMULA-
TION FROM WITHOUT, CAUSES A RESPONSE FROM THE LIFE IN FORM.
"A SON OF GOD IS BORN!"

XIV   Individualisation

Individualisation is the transition from animal consciousness in the third kingdom of nature to self-consciousness in man in the fourth kingdom of nature.

This event of individualisation indicates the appearance of *three divine aspects* in a unit of life in form. "A son of God, a Lord of dedicated . . . Will, is born, and the third divine principle of purposive energy is fused with the other two and brings about an entire reorganisation within the animal form."[1]

Individualisation is a great planetary experiment, which means that when the evolving life within the animal form has reached a sufficient stage of awareness and sentiency, the two already functioning divine aspects or Ray forces of Active Intelligence (Ray III) and Love (Ray II) are strong enough to contact another stream of divine expression, namely Ray I of Will or Power. At

---

"On the third level of the mental plane, the egoic lotus is found and the student should picture it to himself as follows: Concealed at the very center or heart of the lotus is a brilliant point of electric fire of a blue-white hue (the jewel in the lotus) surrounded, and completely hidden, by three closely folded petals. Around this central nucleus, or inner flame, are arranged the nine petals in circles of three petals each, making three circles in all. These petals are formed out of the substance of the solar angels . . . —substance which is not only sentient . . . but which has an added quality of 'I-ness' or self-consciousness, enabling the spiritual unity at the center . . . to acquire knowledge, awareness, and self-realisation. These nine petals are of a predominant orange hue, though the six other colours are found as secondary colours in a varying degree. The inner three petals are of a lovely lemon-yellow hue. At the base of the lotus petals are the three points of light which mark the position of the permanent atoms, which are the medium of communication between the solar Angels and the lunar Pitris. . . . The light within these permanent atoms has a dull red glow."

—*A Treatise on Cosmic Fire*, pp. 761-62.

individualisation it is the higher aspect of Divinity that takes the initiative and causes, through a stimulation from without, a response from the life in form. Today, only the domesticated animals are prepared and waiting for individualisation.[2]

For humanity this great event of individualisation took place 21 million years ago, and instances of coordination between brain and mind occurred about 18 million years ago when man registered his individuality.[3]

Individualisation is literally the coming together of the two factors of spirit and matter by means of a third factor, the intelligent will, purpose, and action of an Entity. Light is produced, a flame shines forth, and a sphere of radiant glory is seen, which gradually increases the intensity of light, its heat, and its radiance until capacity is reached, or what we call perfection.[4]

The impulse from the higher aspect of Divinity comes through the sacrifice of certain cosmic Entities who "offer Themselves" up in order to produce in man self-consciousness and thereby enable the divine spirit to enter into fuller life. This method of individualisation is in our present solar system the result of forces that enter from the cosmic mental plane and sweep into activity those Entities—the solar angels—whose function it is to form the body of the ego out of their own living substance on the mental plane. Thus, through their own quality and nature, they endow human units with the faculty of self-consciousness and both energise and coordinate the minds of all human beings that they may in due time intelligently express the will and purpose of the indwelling Thinker, God Immanent.[5]

At individualisation only a dim outline of a form on mental levels makes its appearance; only faint vibrations are to be seen pulsating in the bud of the egoic lotus. The process of radiant interaction between the lower levels and the higher covers a long period in which the solar angels prepare and work on their own plane to produce the receptacles for the life of God.

After individualisation the human being is at first prey to the illusions of the senses, and his mentality rather hinders and imprisons but finally releases and liberates. Through the life of the senses he consciously experiences his individuality. Then he asserts his individuality through his use of the discriminating mind. And finally he arrives at the ultimate sacrifice of that individuality to the group.

When the animal kingdom had reached a particular stage of development, there was an inrush into the planetary Life of the energy of all the Seven Rays simultaneously, and this tremendous stimulation produced the emergence of infant humanity. It is the pouring in of a triple energy in seven ways that makes it possible for a new kingdom to appear. It was the reaction of that kingdom as expressed through its indwelling life, the animal Being, which produced individualisation in the more advanced animal-man at the time.[6]

Egos of all Ray types individualised upon the moon chain, and the egos of Active Intelligence constituted 75 percent of all incarnated egos, with the remaining 25 percent divided between the other two Rays—Love and Will. In Lemurian times, egos of Love-Wisdom constituted 75 percent of all egos, with the remaining 25 percent on the third Ray of Active Intelligence. In early Atlantean days a large influx of the Power-Will type individualised; 80 percent who entered the human evolution were egos expressing the will aspect of Deity, and 20 percent were along the line of Love-Wisdom. All these, plus the egos that individualised upon the moon chain, constitute the bulk of our modern humanity.[6]

The now self-conscious human beings became gradually aware of a greater world that they lived in. And consciously or unconsciously, all human beings recognise God Transcendent and God Immanent, God greater than the whole, yet God present also in the part. God Transcendent guarantees the Plan for our world, conditioning all lives from the minutest atom, through all the kingdoms of nature, to mankind.[7]

Today we take our stand upon the belief of the innate rightness of the human; we believe in God Immanent, for God Transcendent eternally exists. But He can only be seen and known and correctly approached by God Immanent—immanent in individual men and women, in groups, and in nations.[8]

Christ was the first of our Earth humanity to achieve the goal of God-consciousness, whereas the Buddha was the last of the moon-chain humanity to do so.

On the level of the Soul, we ourselves as souls took human bodies with deliberation and full understanding in order to make possible the evolution of the indwelling consciousness of Deity, which had worked its way through the subhuman kingdoms in nature and needed the activity of the solar angels to make further progress possible. Herein lies our service to God, to other souls, and to other forms of life in other kingdoms.[6]

This evolution of the individual consciousness in human beings occurs in stages of soul growth. Human beings will be found at every stage of consciousness. In one, the emphasis will be upon the sensory life. In some, the consciousness will shift emphasis from one vehicle to another. Others will be ready for full expression as an integrated personality, but working for material ends.

There will be those who awaken to a higher sense of values, shifting their focus of attention out of the world of selfish living into that of true spiritual realities. Little by little, the consciousness of the third aspect of Divinity is coordinated with that of the second aspect, and the Christ-consciousness is aroused into activity through the experience in form. To the gained personality experience is added the intuitive spiritual perception, which is the heritage of those who are awake within the kingdom of God. Paralleling this development of the consciousness in man is the evolution of the instruments whereby that consciousness is brought into rapport with a rapidly expanding world of sensory perception, of intellectual concepts, and of intuitive recognitions.[6]

NOTES

1. *Esoteric Psychology* I, p. 258.
2. Ibid., pp. 259–61.
3. *A Treatise on White Magic*, pp. 440–41.
4. *A Treatise on Cosmic Fire*, pp. 343–45.
5. Ibid., pp. 707–18. See also *Esoteric Psychology* II, pp. 92–96.
6. *Esoteric Psychology* II, pp. 92–93, 210–12, 335–39.
7. *Reappearance of the Christ*, pp. 144–45.
8. *Glamour, a World Problem*, p. 162.

XV. HUMANITY, AS THE FOURTH KINGDOM OF NATURE, CONSTI-
TUTES—LIKE EVERY OTHER KINGDOM—A TOTALITY OF LIVES.

XV Rays and the Human Kingdom

Humanity is the fourth kingdom in nature. It constitutes, like every other kingdom, a totality of lives. Just as the myriad of atomic and cell lives constitute man's body, so it is with the greater life that informs mankind as a whole. Humanity is a living entity occupying a physical form. The rays that predominantly govern the evolution of consciousness in humanity are *Ray IV* (orange) *Harmony through Conflict* and *Ray V* (green) *Science or Concrete Knowledge.*

These two major influences—harmony through conflict and the power to achieve knowledge through discriminating choice—sweep through humanity as a whole and drive it forward to its divine destiny, for humanity is the treasure house of God. Only in the human kingdom are the three divine qualities—Will or Power, Love-Wisdom, and Active Intelligence—found in their full flower and together.

To men and women is given the privilege to reveal the nature of divine consciousness and what is hidden in the Mind of God. And to men and women is given the task to raise matter up to heaven through conscious manifestation of divine power. Divinity, however, must be lived, loved, expressed, and manifested in order to be intellectually grasped.

The past glory of *individualisation* must fade away in that of *initiation*. The slowly emerging self-consciousness must be lost sight of in the wonder of group consciousness. We define a human being essentially as a trinity—Spirit, soul, body; or Monad, ego, personality. Humanity is likewise a Monad, with seven egoic ray groups, within which all souls in and out of incarnation find their place. These seven ray groups manifest in corresponding racial forms, through which the seven groups of souls cyclically express themselves.

All souls work out their destiny in all races, but certain types predominate in certain racial forms. When we realize this truth—that all of us at some time experience incarnation in all racial forms—we see only unity. And when we see humanity itself as an integrated entity in which every human being is a cell, where is there room for racial antipathies?

The influences of the fourth Ray of Harmony, Beauty, Unity, and of the fifth Ray of Concrete Knowledge, or the power to know, sweep through humanity and increasingly govern the power of man's mental life. The fifth Ray is responsible for the development of the intellect, and the fourth Ray eventually produces the appearance of the intuition. Human beings can count on, and infallibly depend upon, these predisposing factors. They guarantee attainment but also bring about turmoil. Harmony, expressing itself in beauty and creative power, is gained through battle, stress, and strain. Knowledge, expressing itself eventually through wisdom, is attained only through the agony of successively presented choices. And these, submitted to the discriminating intelligence during the process of life experience, finally produce the sense of true values, the vision of the ideal, and the capacity to distinguish reality by penetrating the veils of glamour and illusion.

What is proven true on a small scale opens the door to an understanding of what exists on larger scales in planetary, solar, and cosmic realms. Humanity is rapidly integrating the three aspects of human nature, thereby becoming better able to respond to both the cosmic Ray of the solar system—the Ray of Love-Wisdom—and the cosmic personality Ray of the planetary Logos—the Ray of Active Intelligence—the Being in whom we live and move and have our being.

"The secret of the quality of humanity . . . is the power to identify the human consciousness with all other forms of consciousness and of awareness, with all forms of unconscious and instinctual response, and with all forms of the superconscious or divine sense of being." When, through right knowledge, complete harmony is achieved, the fourth kingdom will have entered the fifth kingdom in nature, the kingdom of the Soul.[1]

NOTES

1. See *Esoteric Psychology* I, pp. 311-48.

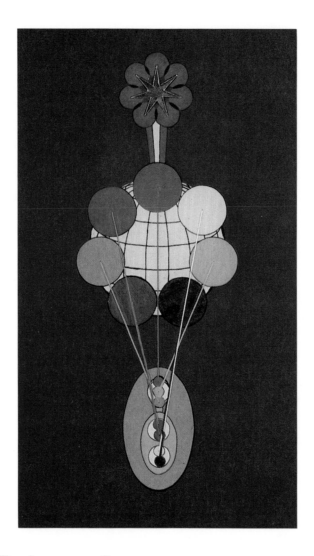

XVI. *The Individual Being* is a living son of god, occupying an animal body. The secret of the human quality is
the power to identify with all other forms of consciousness
and awareness, with all forms of unconscious and instinctual response. This includes identification with all forms of
the superconscious or divine sense of being.

XVI   Rays and the Individual Human Being

A human being is a living son of God (a soul) occupying an animal body. We unify in ourselves the results of the evolution of consciousness of the past and the process of a new factor, that of an individual self-sustaining, self-knowing aspect. This unity produces a consciousness of self-awareness and of immortality. This new factor, however, must be developed. It has been and is developing with great rapidity today. Human activity has reached an incredible speed and intensity and indicates the rapid integration of the three aspects of nature (physical, emotional, mental) into a personality.[1]

For the greater part of our life experience we are governed first sequentially, then simultaneously, by the Ray that governs our physical body, then by the Ray that influences our emotional nature, and then by the Ray that controls the mental nature. When these three are aligned, the *personality Ray* emerges and the three body Rays become subordinated to it. Then the *Soul Ray*, or egoic Ray, begins to work and, as it becomes eventually dominant, the other Rays become subordinated, and the soul-conscious human being can use the personality aspects at will.[2]

Each individual human being is subject to a large number of Ray influences that play upon him, form him, and make him the complexity he is:

1   The solar Ray of Love-Wisdom.

2   The planetary Ray of Active Intelligence.

3   The Rays of humanity as a whole, Harmony through Conflict, and of Science.

4   The Ray of his own soul, which may be any one of the Seven Rays.

71

> 5 The Ray of his own personality, which may be any one of
>   the Seven Rays.[3]

An Analysis of the Seven Rays and Their Expression When Applied to Man

Ray I of Will or Power

People on this Ray have strong will power for either good or evil; for good when the will is directed by wisdom and made selfless by love. The first ray person will always "come to the front." He or she is the born leader, one to trust and lean on, one to defend the weak. He or she is fearless of consequences and utterly indifferent to comment. But if not modified by wisdom and love, a first ray person can be of unrelenting cruelty and hardness of nature. A first ray person often has strong feelings, loves strong contrasts and masses of flowers, but is seldom an artist himself. He or she delights in great orchestral effects, and, if modified by other Rays, may be a great composer. The literary work of a first ray person will be strong and trenchant, but with little care for style or finish. First ray people take the kingdom of heaven "by violence."

Some of their special virtues are: strength, courage, truthfulness, fearlessness, and the capacity to grasp great questions in a large-minded way. Some of the drawbacks are: pride and ambition, willfulness, arrogance, and the desire to control others.

Ray II of Love-Wisdom

Ray II is called the Ray of wisdom because of its characteristic desire for pure knowledge and truth. When power and love are present, we have the ray nature of great teachers of humanity; if without love, the attitude may be cold and selfish. Because of the tendency to tact and foresight, a person on the second Ray will make a first-rate teacher, or an excellent ambassador, and will have the capacity to impress others with true views of things. Combined with other Rays, the second ray person makes a good business executive. If an artist, he or she will seek to teach through art; if a writer, the literary work will be instructive. The Path will be approached through earnest study of the teaching until the intellectual knowledge becomes a spiritual rule of living, which brings in the intuition and true wisdom.

The second ray person will have patience and endurance, love of truth, calmness and strength, faithfulness, intuition, and clear intelligence. Some drawbacks are: overabsorption in study, coldness and indifference to others, and contempt of mental limitation perceived in others.

Ray III of Active Intelligence or Higher Mind

This is the ray of the abstract thinker, the philosopher, the person who delights in higher mathematics; but unless modified by a more practical Ray, he would hardly bother to keep his accounts accurately. He can grasp the essence of a truth and from his wider views see clearly every side of a question. He will make a good businessman. The subject of his artistry will be full of thought and interest, but technically not fine. The third ray person will love music but seldom produce it. He is full of ideas but is often too impractical to carry them out. One type of this Ray is to a degree unpunctual, slovenly, and idle, but if influenced by the fifth Ray may make the truly great mathematician who soars into heights of abstract thought and yet can bring the results down to practical, scientific use. He or she can be a master of the pen. The method of approach to the great Quest is that of deep thinking until one is led to the great Beyond and to the treading of the Path that leads there.

The third ray person will have wide views on abstract questions, sincerity of purpose, capacity for concentration on philosophic studies, and patience. He will not worry over trifles. Some of the drawbacks are intellectual pride, coldness, inaccuracy in details, selfishness, and overmuch criticism of others.

Ray IV of Harmony through Conflict, or the "Ray of Struggle"

On this ray the qualities of activity and inertia are so strangely equal in proportion that one is torn between the two. Inertia follows the path of least resistance. The fourth ray person loves ease and pleasure, to let things go and take no thought of tomorrow. Yet the ever present urge to action is fiery and impatient. These contrasting forces make life one of perpetual warfare and unrest. But the experience gained thereby may produce a rapid evolution. It is the Ray of the person full of enthusiasm and plans, of the speculator and gambler, overwhelmed by sorrow or failure, but just as quickly recovering from reverses. If an artist, the colour is always great, for he or she loves colour, although the drawing may often be defective. The fourth ray person is full of melody and loves a tune. As a writer, he will produce work often brilliant and picturesque, yet full of exaggeration and often pessimistic. The fourth ray person varies between brilliant conversation and gloomy silences and is a delightful but difficult person to live with.

Some of the strong points of a person on the fourth ray are: generosity, sympathy, strong affections and devotion, quickness of perception, and physical courage. But the fourth ray person often lacks moral courage, is often self-centered, inaccurate, extravagant, and given to worries.

Ray V of Concrete Knowledge or Lower Mind

Ray V is the Ray of science and research. The person on this Ray will possess a keen intellect, great awareness of detail, and will spare no effort to verify every theory. Generally, he or she is extremely truthful and full of lucid explanations of facts but can sometimes be pedantic and wearisome because of insistence on trivial details. This is the Ray of the great chemist, the first-rate engineer, the great operating surgeon, one who would make an excellent head of some special technical department. Their writing or speaking will be clarity itself but may lack fire and point and will often be long-winded. The method of approaching the Path is through scientific research pushed to ultimate conclusions and accepting the inferences that follow.

Some of the strong points are strictly accurate statements, justice, perseverance, common sense, uprightness, independence, and keen intellect. Some of the drawbacks are narrowness, harsh criticism, prejudice, and lack of sympathy and reverence.

Ray VI of Devotion and Idealism

The person on the sixth Ray is full of religious instincts and must have a "personal God," a Deity to adore. Everything is either perfect or intolerable; friends are either angels or the opposite, depending on their reaction to his or her favorite idols. The best type of this Ray makes the saint, the worst the fanatic. Sixth ray people will lay down their lives for the object of their devotion but may not lift a finger to help those outside their own sympathies. They will not be great statesmen or good businessmen but may be great preachers or orators. They are devoted to beauty, colour, and all things lovely, but unless influenced by the fourth or seventh Ray, their productive skills are not great. They love melodious music and may compose sacred music. Their way of approaching the Path would be by prayer and meditation, aiming at union with God.

Devotion, love, tenderness, loyalty, and reverence are some of their special virtues. Some of their drawbacks are selfish and jealous love, partiality, prejudice, and over-rapid conclusions.

Ray VII of Ceremonial Magic and Order

Ray VII is the Ray that makes a person delight in "all things done decently and in order" and according to rule and precedent. It is the Ray of the high priest, the genius in organisation, the perfect nurse for the sick, careful in the smallest detail, although sometimes too much inclined to disregard the patient's idiosyncrasies. It is the Ray of the perfect sculptor and designer of beautiful forms. Combined with fourth ray characteristics, it would make the very highest type of artist, form and colour being particularly excellent.

The seventh ray person would always be fluent in writing and speech, and the writer would be more concerned about the polished style than the matter he was writing about. The seventh ray person will delight in great processions and shows, as well as in genealogical trees and rules of precedence, and is determined to do the right thing at the right moment, which makes for great social success.

On the other hand, superstitions and deep interest in omens, dreams, and spiritualistic phenomena are serious drawbacks. Strong points are strength, perseverance, courtesy, extreme care in details, and self-reliance. Weak points are formalism, bigotry, narrowness, superficial judgement, and over-indulged self-opinion.

Some of the Rays are more closely related to one or another of the other six Rays. There is a close relationship between the third and fifth Rays in the search after knowledge. The correspondence between the second and sixth Rays makes for the intuitive grasp of synthesised knowledge and the common bond of faithfulness and loyalty. Masterfulness, steadfastness, and perseverance are the corresponding characteristics of the first and seventh ray combination.[4]

The human entity is a curious synthesis on the subjective side of his nature, producing a fusion of life, power, harmonious intent, and mental activity. The following summarises the Rays that govern and differentiate the *life of the personality:*

Rays I, IV, and V	predominate in the life of humanity and govern with increasing power a person's *mental life* and determine the mental body.
Rays II and VI	potently govern the *emotional life* and determine the type of the astral body.
Rays III and VII	govern the vital, *physical life* and the physical body.[5]

But the egoic or soul Ray gradually negates the Rays governing the personality. This process causes a detachment from the form side of manifestation and attachment to the formless side of manifestation, which induces group-consciousness and awareness of the subjective whole.

NOTES

1. See *Esoteric Psychology* I, pp. 311–13.
2. Ibid., pp. 333–39, 402–3.
3. Ibid., pp. 404–8.
4. Ibid., pp. 200–13; also *Esoteric Psychology* II, pp. 36–44.
5. Ibid., pp. 320–21.

XVII. *Consciousness Develops in Cycles* that proceed from individualisation to the fully developed self-conscious personality, then through the path of initiation to full soul-consciousness, and finally to identification with the whole, the one, or god.

When they are seen holistically, we can differentiate three stages of growth in the development of consciousness:

XVII   The Way of Consciousness Development

In the human kingdom consciousness develops in cycles and unfolds spirally from individualisation to the fully developed, self-conscious personality. From there it moves through the path of initiation to full soul-consciousness, and finally to identification with the ONE or God. This process takes a very long time, and in its course all Seven Rays powerfully influence humanity as a whole and each human being individually.

While a human being progresses spirally from lower to ever higher and more-inclusive stages of conscious awareness, the cycles depend on the predominating ray influences. These different stages often overlap and interrelate with parallel activity

---

First Stage   The three types of energy—vital, emotional, and mental—blend in the personality into the personality Ray. What has so far been a reflection of the higher Triad becomes now transmuted into the energies of the Soul. This Higher Triad consists of spiritual activity, pure reason, and purpose—Atma, Buddhi, Manas.

Second Stage   On the higher mental planes of the personality, the activities of intelligence and the spiritual activities of the higher mind, which convey illumination, interact. The energy of pure reason, or the intuitive nature, which confers spiritual perception, transforms the self-centered desires of the personality into soul or group consciousness. Eventually, the first aspect of the Higher Triad, that of Will or Purpose, which is divine livingness, dominates the entire expression of the human being. Then he or she is a completely soul-infused being, or a Master who can work with facility in the worlds of the personality as well as in the world of the Soul. The world of the Higher Triad becomes the world of inspiration, and the other the world of service.

Third Stage   This is the expansion of consciousness into solar and cosmic realms, into dimensions we cannot grasp as yet. Who knows where it will end?

taking place. Therefore no hard and fast rules, but only strong indications, can be given.

The development of consciousness in the personality life culminates in the full expression of the personal self, when the energies of the vital, emotional, and mental bodies become blended and fused into one personality Ray, which is often the third aspect of Divinity. Then the fully self-conscious, self-assertive human being comes increasingly under the influences of the dual energy of Love and Will or Purpose—the second and first aspects of Divinity. When these two soul Rays dominate the energies of the personality, they produce the perfect human being. In time the Soul, ever being group-conscious, begins to blend with Life Itself, becoming absorbed into the Supreme Reality. Identification takes place, and God-consciousness—the goal of the self-conscious human being—has been reached.

This definition of a triple expansion of consciousness—Individualisation, Initiation, Identification—is, however, only a temporary definition and may later, with deeper insight, be seen quite differently. Our expansion of consciousness continues into spheres of which we today know nothing.[1] But the greater awareness will always include the lesser awareness. Consequently, all atoms, reactions, identifications, all ray impulses and qualities are included in what will later become the natural state of being.[2]

NOTES

1. See *Esoteric Psychology* II, pp. 8–21.
2. Ibid., pp. 31–32, 49–60.

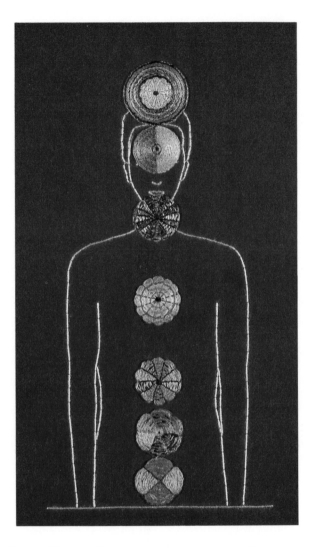

XVIII. *Seven Force Centers* in the vital or "etheric" body.
Underlying the human body in all its parts is the vital or
"etheric" body with its seven major points of focus. All
seven are perpetually rotating wheels into which the life
streams enter that come from and through our solar and
planetary entities.

Illustration based on The Chakras, *by C. W. Leadbeater.*

82

XVIII   Seven Centers in the Human Being

How Does the Soul or Divine Thinker Operate?
Our personality is but the mechanism that the Soul uses to express itself. This occurs in two ways. The "thread of life" is anchored in the heart and functions through the bloodstream, and the "thread of consciousness" or of intelligence is anchored in the head and directs the physical-plane activities through the medium of the brain and the nervous system.

From our point of view, the Soul is ageless, and its activity depends on the point of development of the form in which it operates. This form, in turn, is a reflection of the Soul or Divine Thinker. The Soul, therefore, which operates under the influences of cosmic, solar, and planetary energies and forces, is responsible for the type of brain, the type of mental reaction, and the character with which a given subject enters into incarnation.

Underlying the human body in all its parts is a vehicle called the vital or "etheric" body. It is composed entirely of threads of force. These threads interpenetrate the entire body and the nervous system and are in reality the activating power of the nervous system. This etheric body has within it seven main points of focus called "force centers," which form the major response apparatus for emanations coming from close and distant sources. It is upon these force centers that the life expression and experience of the Soul depends, and not upon the body. [1]

These main force centers in the etheric body are:

1   The center at the base of the spine with four spokes or petals.

2   The sacral center with six spokes or petals.

3   The solar plexus with ten petals.

4   The heart center with twelve petals.

5   The throat center with sixteen petals.

6   The center between the eyebrows—ajna center—with 96 petals.

7   The head center at the very top of the head with 12 major petals and 960 secondary petals, arranged around the central 12, making a total of 972.

The combination of the petals of the sixth and seventh centers is often referred to as the *thousand-petalled Lotus*.

These seven whirlpools of force swirl etheric, astral, and mental matter into activity. Their development to maximum capacity takes a long time. While the individual is under the influence of the personality Ray, the activity aspect becomes developed. As life after life slips away, the human being comes more and more under the control of the intellect by means of the brain, first working through the four minor Rays and coming eventually upon the third Ray, that of Intelligent Activity.

During the period in which the egoic Ray holds sway, the human being throws his forces on the side of evolution, the life becomes disciplined, and the aspirant steps upon the Path of Probation. This continues up to the third initiation, proceeding from the third Ray to one of the sub-rays of the other two major Rays, unless the third Ray is the egoic Ray. The egoic Ray is a direct reflection of the Monad and can be any one of the three Rays of Aspect.[2]

All seven centers are like perpetually rotating wheels into which the life-streams enter that come from our Solar Logos—the second Ray of Love-Wisdom in its seven sub-rays—all of which operate in each of the centers, although one usually predominates. Their light and radiation depend on the point of development that a person has reached. These predominating Rays are:

Head Center: Ray I, Will or Power

Brow Center: Ray V, Concrete Knowledge

Throat Center: Ray III, Active Intelligence

Heart Center: Ray II, Love-Wisdom

Solar Plexus: Ray VI, Devotion

Sacral Center: Ray VII, Ceremonial Magic

Base of the Spine: Ray IV, Harmony[3]

The development of our consciousness is directly related to the activity of the centers within our etheric body.

These centers of expression, through which the soul gains needed experience and becomes sensitive to, and conscious within, the worlds of being (otherwise unknown) have come into manifestation as the result of the "wish" or the desire of the soul. It is the "wish-life" of the soul and not the frustrations of the personality that have brought about the situation with which mankind is contending today.

The right appropriation of form by the soul is the result of an initial wish or desire, a fundamental outgoing impulse on the part of the center of energy. In sensitive awareness lie the secrets of progress for the psyche and the secret of the many states of consciousness that the soul experiences on the path of evolution as it expands its contacts, its influence, and its activities.[4]

The soul unfoldment in the human kingdom was and is a step-by-step shifting of consciousness from:

1 that of the purely physical appetite to the vital, personal being.

2 that of the vital primitive being into desire for material satisfaction.

3 that of the vital emotional desire-emphasis into that of a mental consciousness.

4 that of alternating emphasis in these lower aspects into that of an integrated personality.

5 that of an effective and powerful personality to that of a dimly sensed reality and an awakening to new and higher values.

6 that of shifting its focus of attention out of the world of material, selfish living into that of true spiritual realities.

7 that of gained personality experience into the intuitive, spiritual perceptions.

Paralleling this development of consciousness in the individual human being is the evolution of the instrument by which that consciousness is brought into rapport with a rapidly expanding world of sensory perception, intellectual concepts, and intuitive recognition. As the consciousness expands from stage to stage, the centers in the etheric body awaken and develop "from the closed bud to that of the opened lotus." The petals of the lotus become vibrant and alive and "the jewel in the lotus" also becomes actively alive.

Today, in the Aryan race, the centers in a person's etheric body awaken in three major stages:

1   The throat center awakens, and much of the lower energies is shifted into the throat activity. The "closed bud" opens into that of the "opened lotus."

2   The petals become vibrant and active during the personality integration. The centers below the diaphragm are the controlling factors until the solar plexus becomes the great clearing house for all the lower forces and these lower forces shift into a higher body, the astral body. Throat and eyebrow (ajna) centers become active and produce integrated and creative personalities.

3   Then the heart center awakens, and solar plexus energies shift into it, producing group-consciousness and entering into a new and fuller sense of spiritual energy. During the final stages upon the Path, the heart of the lotus, "the jewel in the lotus," becomes actively alive. The emphasis is then on those states of awareness that reveal the Kingdom of God, and the fifth kingdom of nature becomes creatively active on earth.

The ray types of the vehicles steadily emerge. While at first the personality Ray controls life and then the soul Ray dominates the personality Ray and subdues its activity, eventually the head center awakens, and with it rises the fire of the kundalini at the base of the spine. Body and Soul become integrated, leading to a perfected humanity upon earth. The monadic ray takes control, absorbing into itself the rays of the personality and the soul. The duality is overcome and "only the ONE Who Is remains."[5]

There is a technique of integration for each of the Seven Rays, with the soul acting essentially as the integrating factor. This shows in the early and unconscious stages as the power to hold the forms together in incarnation. In later and conscious stages, it shows as the power of unification of the personality. But human beings cannot avail themselves of these methods of control until they have become integrated within themselves. Then each Ray and its work in integrating the personality will be conveyed by means of a formula of integration, its dual application and rebuilding, and finally the process of alignment of the three bodies. Passing through a crisis of evocation, the person enters a phase of light where he or she clearly sees the next step to be taken and receives the revelation of the Plan and what each one has to do.

NOTES

1. See *Esoteric Psychology* II, pp. 62–70.
2. See *A Treatise on Cosmic Fire*, pp. 161–79.
3. See *Esoteric Psychology* I, p. 428.
4. See *Esoteric Psychology* II, pp. 318–52.
5. See *A Treatise on Cosmic Fire*, pp. 558–61, 708–14.

XIX. *The Spiritual Government of Our Planet Earth.*
Three major centers constitute the spiritual government of
our earth through which the planetary logos functions.
These centers are:

XIX   The Spiritual Government of Our Planet Earth

This illustration of the spiritual government of our Earth is based on Master Djwhal Khul's teachings about our world. It represents in symbols the three major groups of beings who are responsible for the manifestation of the divine Plan on earth. The purpose of this plan is to make our planet through the processes of evolution, renewal, and resurrection into a sacred planet. The three inter-related groups or centers are: *Shamballa,* the *Hierarchy,* and *Humanity.*

1 Shamballa consists of the Lord of the World and His Council, with Sanat Kumara presiding, who came to our planet eighteen million years ago.[1] It is in Shamballa that the living will of the Unknown God is seen in completeness and already exists.[2] This great Unknown Being, our Planetary Logos ("lotus blossom with flaming center") focuses in and through the Individuality of Sanat Kumara ("eye below the lotus") as, by analogy, the soul of a human being uses a temporary personality when that personality is of an advanced stage of initiate consciousness.

This center of the Lord of the World and His Council is characterized by Divinity, and Divinity is the expression of the Will or Purpose of the ONE in Whom we live and move and have our being. It is the center where the Will of God is focused and dynam-

---

1. THE LORD OF THE WORLD AND HIS COUNCIL, OFTEN CALLED SHAMBALLA.

2. THE HIERARCHY, THE FIFTH KINGDOM OF NATURE, A SOCIETY OF ILLUMINED MINDS.

3. HUMANITY IN ITS VARIOUS STAGES OF CONSCIOUSNESS DEVELOPMENT FROM THE UNEVOLVED TO THE NEW GROUP OF WORLD SERVERS.

ically sent forth to carry out that purpose. Sanat Kumara is to the planetary Logos what the personality plus the soul is to the disciple. He is also the coherent force within the planet, holding through His radiatory influence all forms and all substances in the planetary form so that they constitute one coherent, energised, and functioning whole.[3]

The basic purpose of Sanat Kumara is to bring about right relations in every field of His manifested life. Today, for the first time, the activity of humanity itself is concerned with the entire subject of right human relations and how to bring them about, which means that today, also for the first time, humanity is consciously responding to the will and intention of Shamballa, even without realizing the esoteric implications.[4]

Forming the innermost circle of the Council of the Lord of the World is a group of Lives Who—although not as far advanced as He—are yet greatly in advance of the most highly developed members of the spiritual Hierarchy. Their normal contacts are extraplanetary and are in direct rapport with the Planetary Logos upon His high plane, the cosmic mental plane.[5] Many of these greater Lives Who work in the Council Chamber of Sanat Kumara found Their way to our planet from our sister planet Venus, thereby establishing enduring relationships.[6]

Members of the Great Council, among others, are the three Buddhas of Activity ("the three crowns") and the Seven Spirits before the Throne of God, who are in close rapport with the seven sacred planets in our solar system.[7] These Seven Spirits are reflections of the Lords of the Rays—the seven sub-rays of the second Cosmic Ray—constituting three rays of aspect and four rays of attribute.

One great Buddha of Activity is responsible to Sanat Kumara for the Plan's working out in connection with humanity. His two Brothers have each of Them an equally important responsibility and have their own Hierarchies to work through. One works with the Deva Kingdom and the other with the three subhuman Kingdoms of Nature.[8] The Council Chamber of the Lord of Shamballa is a unit, and the Hierarchy is a differentiation of this basic unity.

2 The Hierarchy is the second major center in the spiritual government of our world, with three departmental heads: The Manu—Will—first Ray; the Mahachohan, the Lord of Civilisation—Active Intelligence—third Ray; the Bodhisattva, the Christ or World Teacher—Love-Wisdom—second Ray ("three stars within the triangle"); and various Masters heading the specific major ashrams, with their subsidiary ashrams headed by Initiates and Disciples.[9]

In the consciousness of Sanat Kumara, the Hierarchy constitutes "the noble middle Path" to which the Buddha refers. It fills the intermediate and the mediating place between Shamballa and Humanity. It is one great ashram, and after due absorption of light, understanding, and power from Shamballa, it radiates this energy to aid not only the human evolution but all the other evolutions as well. This great ashram is likewise magnetic in its effect. Through its magnetic potency, "units of life and devotion"—human beings—are brought into the ashram as disciples. This great ashram is composed of many ashrams, and the Christ, aided by the Manu and the Mahachohan, is the coordinator of the entire life of it. The personnel of the ashram is today entirely provided from the ranks of humanity.

There are seven major ray ashrams and forty-two secondary ashrams that are gradually forming. The entire hierarchical ashram is a unity and is guarded by its radiation. The forty-two lesser ashrams are held together by the magnetic interaction of the whole. Aspirants are drawn into the ashram through radiation. There is a dual flow of energy into the great ashram. This dual flow consists of:

1 *the energizing life from Shamballa.*

2 *the energy of active intelligence from Humanity*, thus enabling the Masters to formulate the Plan. It is the admixture of love and will that produces radiation. It is the Hierarchy's conscious use of the power coming from Shamballa that results in the magnetic impact and the spiritual "pull"

that draws the soul, incarnated in the body, towards the ashram.

The keynote of working in an ashram is complete freedom from all coercion within the ashram and from any supervision of daily activity and instinctive reaction to the ray influences and to the "breath of the prevailing will." Today pure reason or true love is beginning to manifest itself through the quality of all the Rays functioning through their respective ashram. The secondary ray quality will serve to implement the expression of pure love, which is the primary quality of the Lord of the World, Sanat Kumara.

The Plan is the expression of the Purpose or the Will of God, and it is the service of the Plan that binds the seven ashrams and their subsidiary ashrams into a great whole. But it is the potency of the Shamballic magnetism that evokes the will or first ray nature, inherent in every human being, which unfolds consciously only within the periphery of the great ashram. What really implements the Plan is the focussed, dynamic, and energising will energy at the heart of the Hierarchy, coming from Shamballa.

3 Humanity constitutes the third major center in the spiritual world government. Today all three centers interrelate and demonstrate great activity (indicated by the blue ribbon, running through all three centres). Shamballa, Hierarchy, and Humanity are much more closely related than ever before and are now ready to enter into a new historical period. In this coming cycle, D. K. says, we shall see the first stages of great spiritual fusion taking form in the externalisation of the ashram, so that the Hierarchy and Humanity will meet and know each other. When these two centers can work in full cooperation, then Shamballa will take form and no longer exist only in cosmic etheric substance.

All this is to be brought about through the invocative spirit of mankind plus the initiatory process carried on in the ashram. Much lies hidden in the free will and right timing of human beings. But the future of spiritual cooperation and interplay within and without the great ashram is assured. Today the world situation is one of great interest. Humanity is ready for a great step forward towards a conscious approach to more spiritual living. And the Hierarchy is orienting itself to a much closer rapport with humanity.[10]

Every human being is intended to be the intelligent arbiter of his own destiny and a conscious exponent of his own innate divinity, of the God within.[11] There are many within the human family who in conscious awareness build the bridge between Humanity and Hierarchy. All men and women of goodwill in every country are on the way to serve the Plan. If each nation will first see the importance of attending to its own internal problems and beautify its national life by producing order, stabilisation, and above all freedom, then cooperation and a reciprocal interplay in the field of economics can come about. Basic human needs must be met in order to usher in the deeply desired peace and plenty.

The growth of the group idea with its emphasis upon group good, group understanding, group interrelation, and goodwill shall lead to that universal goodwill that enables a person in any country to identify with his or her brothers and sisters in other parts of the world. Human beings are innately kind when their minds are not distorted or their visions impaired by selfish interests. By our thinking in terms of goodwill for the whole, and not only the good of certain sections within the national life or certain nations at the expense of other sections or nations, this universal goodwill shall enhance and eventually bring about worldwide, national, religious, and economic interdependence. Such organisations as World Goodwill, the United Nations (in its various agencies, such as UNESCO and UNICEF), the World Federalists, Planetary Citizens, and many other groups of concerned thinkers and scientists are today extending great efforts to find workable and inspired solutions to the many problems facing every nation. All of this indicates an expansion of consciousness and greater inclusiveness.

Some of these men and women of goodwill with their clarity of vision and understanding will be the interpreters of the newer and truer values and ideas that always aim at the production of worldwide goodwill, of intelligent and loving understanding and unity. They will work for right human relations, for the basic oneness of humanity, for practical brotherhood, and for positive harmlessness in speech and writing. They will also recognise the value of the individual, as well as the significance of group work.

Once this mass consciousness is evoked and functioning, a stabilised opinion will be possible—one so strong that in every country acts of cruelty, oppression, war, personal ambition, enforced obedience through penalties, and selfish aggrandisement at the expense of the helpless will no longer be tolerated.[12] This avantgarde is known as the New Group of World Servers and exists unorganised in every country.[13]

It seems that all our life is relationships to energies and forces emanating from any one of these three major centres of our world government, energies we can learn to know, to contact, to control, and lead into directions of greater freedom, greater beauty and truth. It is really up to each of us what we do with our life. Influences penetrate from all directions, positive and negative, helpful and destructive. We ourselves must decide to which of these energies and forces we want to respond.

The three centres of our spiritual world government are basically an expression of states of consciousness:

The Human Consciousness is awareness of the Soul within the form; recognition and cooperation with the Soul, Intelligence, Action, Expression—the influence of the consecrated personality.

The Hierarchical Consciousness is awareness of the Higher Self, the Soul; recognition and cooperation with Divinity, Love, Attraction, Relation—the influence of the Soul.

The Shamballa Consciousness is awareness of the unity and purpose of Life; recognition and cooperation with the Plan, Will, Direction, Oneness—the influence of the Triad.[14]

The first of the three departments within the spiritual government for which the Hierarchy is responsible is the department of the *Manu* (at this time the Master Morya), Who is concerned with and watches over the governments of the various nations, to the end that right relations in each nation and between all nations may become established. His department is under the influences of the *First Ray of Will or Power.*

The second department is that of the *Christ, the World Teacher,* Who in the East is called the Lord Maitreya. He is concerned with the spiritual destiny of Humanity. He is the head of all major religions and the true spiritual values in all of them, which will be the essence of the New World Religion, which is the Christ-consciousness within each and all of humanity, God Immanent and God Transcendent. The *Second Ray of Love-Wisdom* strongly influences this department.

The third department is that of the *Mahachohan* (at this time Comte de St. Germain). He is the *Lord of Civilisation.* His endeavour is to stimulate the intelligence in human beings so that everyone will seek and appreciate the true, the beautiful, and spiritual values. A major part of his work lies in the direction of stimulating cooperation in place of competition, and in sharing and distribution in place of centralisation. The third department is under the influences of the *Third Ray of Active Intelligence.*

All these ideals strike a familiar note within us, because they express what we as individuals and groups hope to bring about in preparation for the Coming One. The Master D. K. tells us that Christ has always remained with humanity, that He has never left the Earth since His physical presence some 2000 years ago. Now we expect Him to reappear and leave his present retreat in Central Asia.

NOTES

1. *A Treatise on Cosmic Fire*, p. 211.
2. *The Rays and the Initiations*, p. 371.
3. Ibid., pp. 204–6.
4. Ibid., p. 394.
5. Ibid., p. 206.

6. Ibid., p. 379.
7. Ibid., p. 207.
8. Ibid., p. 440.
9. *A Treatise on Cosmic Fire*, p. 1239.
10. *The Rays and the Initiations*, pp. 372–87.
11. *Esoteric Psychology* II, p. 484.
12. Ibid., pp. 652–77.
13. *World Goodwill* (New York: Lucis Trust).
14. *The Rays and the Initiations*, p. 466.

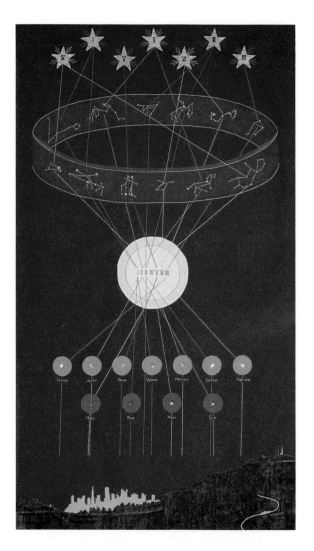

XX. This illustration of *Rays, Constellations, and Planetary Rulers* is based on tabulation v in *Esoteric Astrology*.* It differs from illustration viii, as here only the conditioning ray energies are depicted that primarily influence disciples and initiates, human beings who have reached an advanced stage of consciousness development.

Esoteric Astrology, p. 66.

100

XX Rays Conditioning Disciples and Initiates

Looking at the multitude of glittering stars on a clear night, and knowing that each and billions more are magnificent, intelligent, living Beings—radiating energies in constant interchange throughout the cosmic expanse—our Planet Earth, as one of these heavenly bodies, takes on much greater significance. We can visualise each human being and humanity as a whole as conscious, active participants in this divine manifestation. And the statement "God Immanent, striving ever for recognition, is Itself impelled thereto by the fact of God Transcendent" reveals cosmic, solar, planetary, and personal implications.[1]

This specific and symbolic presentation of fascinating realities, although very incomplete, may give an inkling of the existing interrelations and interactions that exist between cosmic, solar, and planetary energies and forces. Here emphasis is laid on astrological relationships of conditioning ray energies and forces in connection with disciples and initiates. These ray energies, which are sub-rays of the second cosmic Ray of Love-Wisdom—the Ray of our Solar Logos coming from seven stars of the Great Bear, known as Ursa Major, are transmitted to our solar system through certain constellations of the Zodiac, as only our Solar Logos is capable of responding directly to such high-powered energies of the divine Will of God. There transmuted, they become attracted to the different planets in our solar system. The planetary lives in

---

Our Earth is indicated by a view of San Francisco as seen from Shelter Ridge in Mill Valley. Also, the colours, indicating the various streams of energy, differ as they coincide with the colours mentioned in the Secret Doctrine.†

†*Esoteric Psychology* I, pp. 418–21.

turn absorb these energies and radiate them, transfigured, to disciples and initiates on our Earth. Different combinations of ray energies influence and help unfold the consciousness of each human being, as well as of subhuman lives, according to the stage of consciousness development reached.[2]

In relation to our solar system, the seven ray energies become the seven builders, the seven sources of life. They are the original psychic Entities, imbued with the capacity to express Love and to emerge from subjective Being into objective Becoming.[3]

How do these beneficent energies that impel, but do not compel, influence and condition disciples and initiates?

Ray I, the Energy of Will or Power, coming from the Great Bear to our solar system, is transmitted through the constellations Taurus and Pisces. Then, transfigured by the planets Vulcan and Pluto, it effects in the disciple a transmutation of desire into sacrifice, and of the individual will into the divine will, leading to the emergence of a

World Saviour.

Ray II, the Energy of Love-Wisdom, is transmitted through the constellations Leo and Aquarius. Then, absorbed and transfigured by the Sun and Jupiter, it effects in the disciple the development of the individual consciousness into world consciousness, producing a

World Server.

Ray III, the Energies of Active Intelligence, coming into our solar system through the constellations Sagittarius and Capricorn, becomes transmuted and transfigured by Saturn and our planet Earth and influences the one-pointed disciple to become the

Initiate.

Ray IV, the Energy of Harmony through Conflict, reaches our solar system through the constellations Aries and Virgo, and then, transfigured by Mercury and the Moon (hiding a planet), affects the disciple. The influences of this Ray-Life harmonise both the cosmos and the individual through conflict, producing unity and beauty, the birthpangs of the second birth bringing forth the

Cosmic and the Individual Christ.

Ray V, the Energy of Concrete Knowledge and Science, reaches the Sun via the constellation Gemini, becomes absorbed and transfigured by Venus, and so reaches the disciple on Earth. His individualised consciousness becomes subordinate to the consciousness of the group, and the effect is

Liberation through Initiation.

Ray VI, the Energy of Idealism or Devotion, is transmitted through the constellations Cancer and Scorpio and reaches the disciple by way of Neptune and Mars. The influences of this great Ray-Life effect in the disciple the transformation of mass consciousness into the inclusive consciousness of the

Triumphant Disciple.

Ray VII, the Energy of Order, Ceremonial Magic, and Synthesis, enters our solar system by way of Libra and comes to our planet through Uranus, producing a "beneficent organisation" of the totality of energies found in the initiate's equipment. When this reorganisation is complete at the fifth initiation, the initiate can "escape from off the wheel and can then truly live."[4]

The significance for us in this great vision lies in the fact that "the goal of evolution for humanity is to become consciously and livingly aware of the nature of these energies and begin to know them and use them.[5] Even a dim perception of that vast aggregation of Intelligent Forces will serve to bring into clearer light the realisation that our solar system—and consequently our planet Earth—is a part of this immense whole. "Because these forces are, we are; because They persist, we persist; because They move in form and space and time, we do the same."[6]

NOTES

1. *Glamour, a World Problem*, p. 176.
2. See *Esoteric Astrology*, pp. 85, 612, 66-67, 266-67, 609-11.
3. *Esoteric Psychology* I, pp. 22-26.
4. See *Esoteric Astrology*, pp. 65-72, 600-601.
5. Ibid., p. 23.
6. Ibid., pp. 607-9.

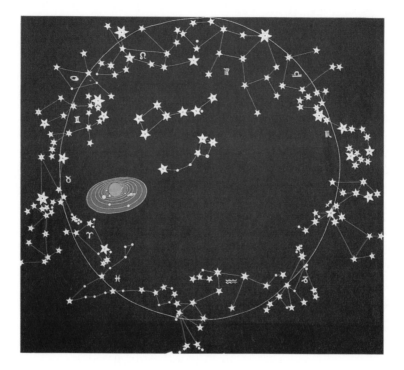

XXI. *Our Zodiac and the Ecliptic*, or the apparent way our sun and its planets travel among the stars in the course of a year (described by the golden circle). The zodiacal symbols of each of the twelve constellations or signs are also indicated.

XXI Our Zodiac

In many places Full Moon meditation meetings are held monthly to contemplate the universe and the energies and forces coming from the constellations of the Zodiac, influencing our solar system, our Earth, our individual consciousness, and to some extent even subconscious states of being throughout the year. These meetings provide an opportunity to acknowledge with joy the beauty and beneficence that Divinity bestows upon us through the streams of energy that radiate to our Earth by way of the Sun from and through these great zodiacal Entities.

Before we consider the deeper significance and the effects of the zodiacal signs upon the development of our consciousness, it may be interesting to visualise the actual existence of the constellations of stars that surround us in space day and night, year in and year out. We need to understand these radiating energies in order to use their powerful blessings in our daily life.

The stars and distances in this illustration are, of course, not to scale, but their location along the *ecliptic* is very close to what we can actually see on clear nights throughout the twelve months of the year. This graphic illustration is based on charts in the book *The Stars*, by H. A. Rey,[1] and shows all of the constellations of the Zodiac as they can be seen from a latitude of about 35° north of the equator. They are: *Aries, Taurus* with Pleiades, *Gemini, Cancer, Leo, Virgo, Libra, Scorpio, Sagittarius, Capricorn, Aquarius,* and *Pisces.* Of course, not all are visible at the same time. At any given moment, about half of them are below the horizon and therefore invisible. Only the so-called circumpolar stars never go below the horizon when seen from this latitude. They include the Big Dipper of the Great Bear and the Little Dipper, with Polaris at the end of its handle.

There are many more constellations dispersed throughout the heavenly vault, but they do not belong to our Zodiac. The Pole Star is a most powerful "Star of Direction." This star, and the two Pointers of the Big Dipper that point directly to the Pole Star, are of great significance in regard to the development of our human consciousness. Nothing in the universe is actually separated; only a beautiful harmony, interrelation, and order exist.

The golden line in this illustration of the Zodiac indicates the ecliptic, which is the apparent way our Sun with its planets travels among the stars within the twelve months of the year. It is called the ecliptic because eclipses of sun and moon occur along this line. As we move along with our Sun in alignment with the constellations of the Zodiac, we do not consider the daily motion of the sky, seen from our Earth at rest; we consider the real yearly motion of the Earth against a sky at rest. Every month our solar system, and we within it, are aligned with a particular constellation. According to the television presentation "Nova—A Whisper from Space," our Sun and its planets move 250 miles per second.

We know from astronomical findings that the distances between the stars are tremendous and are measured by the speed of light. Light travels at the speed of 186,000 miles per second, which is about *11 million miles per minute.* At this rate it takes the light from the Sun to reach our Earth about 8.5 minutes, since the distance from our Earth to the Sun is 93 million miles. The nearest visible star—Alpha Centauri—is 4.5 light-years away. The distances between stars are tremendous; for example, Pollux and Castor in Gemini—the Twins—which appear to us as close neighbors, are in reality 12 light-years apart.[2]

When looking at this illustration, we have to use our imagination and visualise a tremendous universe in which the stars are often billions of miles apart. To get a truer picture of our solar system, let us examine it more closely. The diameter of the Sun is 865,000 miles; of our Earth, 7,926 miles. Every day, our Sun with its planets moves about 1° eastward and completes its ecliptic circle within 365.25 days. We know that the axis around which our planet Earth turns deviates from the vertical by 23.5°, which is responsible for the change of seasons and the various lengths of days and nights. When the Sun in its course along the ecliptic intersects the celestial equator, which happens twice a year, we have the *Spring Equinox* (about 21 March), with the Sun in Pisces, and the *Fall Equinox* (September), when the Sun is in the sign of Virgo.

The Summer and Winter Solstice take place on about 21 June and 22 December, when the Sun begins to move northward. As the planets of our solar system orbit around the Sun, they too can be seen in the starry skies within a belt roughly 18° wide. The Moon, which travels around the Earth, is at New Moon time between the Sun and the Earth, and at Full Moon time the Earth is between the Sun and the Moon. Then the Moon receives the light and radiation from the Sun full force and reflects it back to our Earth.

The stars that compose the various constellations vary in size, degrees of brightness, and magnitude. Among the stars of greatest magnitude in our Zodiac are:

Aldebaran in Taurus   *Regulus in Leo*

Alcyone in the Pleiades of Taurus   *Spica in Virgo*

Pollux and Castor in Gemini   *Antares in Scorpio*

As students we are fortunate to have the books by Alice A. Bailey with a wealth of information about these heavenly Beings inhabiting our universe. Planets, suns, constellations, galaxies, and universes are forms ensouled by magnificent, conscious, evolving Lives—just as on a much smaller scale our consciousness lives in our physical body or form, can roam the realms of our Earth, and is able to expand to ever greater inclusiveness.

We turn now to the deeper, invisible realities, the divine qualities which these great Lives that ensoul the stars, constellations, and our solar system emanate and radiate, and whose radiating streams of energy lead us cycle after cycle from personality-involved human beings to God-like men and women.

But stars do not *compel*, they only *impel* and leave it to our inclinations and our free will to respond.

Through the tremendous network of interrelated energies and forces within the vastness of space, Divinity bestows upon us a wealth of divine qualities, characteristics, and visions of divine purpose by way of radiations coming from the Seven Rays, constellations, our solar system, and our planetary Logos through His three groups that comprise the spiritual government of our world. The book *Esoteric Astrology* and other writings by Alice A. Bailey can give us an overpowering insight into the hidden realities of the great Lives and their specific and beneficent creativity.

The zodiacal Signs themselves, aside from transmitting cosmic ray energies, emit powerful radiations to our solar system and our Earth, of which the following indications are just a few glimpses.

Aries, the Ram, is "The Light of Life Itself." It is the sign of beginnings—the beginning of the creative process; the first step of the soul towards incarnation; the beginning of constant cycles of experience; the beginning wherein the soul changes its direction, its purpose, and its method and finally enters the process of spiritual regeneration and initiation.

The keynotes of the sign of Aries are:

> "Express the will to be and do."
> "Unfold the power to manifest."
> "Enter into battle for the Lord."
> "Arrive at unity through effort."

Aries is the creator of those activities, conditions, and processes that lead to the manifestation of the soul through the medium of form and later to those higher creative undertakings that lead in due time to the manifestation of spirit through the soul.[3]

Taurus, the Bull, becomes the bestower of Light that lightens the darkness of the earlier cycles. Taurus incites towards experience and the gaining of knowledge; and the final stage of development demonstrates as the illumined consciousness. Its basic quality demonstrates as *desire* in the mass of humanity and as *will* or directed purpose in the disciple or initiate. Buddha clarified the nature of desire and its effects. Christ taught the transmutation of desire into aspiration, which is the effort of the human will to conform itself to the will of God in perfect trust.

Now human beings seek another interpretation of God's will— not blind acquiescence and unavoidable acceptance but understanding cooperation with the divine Plan and an enlightened fusion of the individual will with the great divine will, and this for the greater good of the whole. The entire secret of divine purpose and planning is hidden in this sign. The onward rush of the "Bull of God" reveals steadily and without cessation the stupendous and sublime Plan of Deity.

The keynotes of the sign of Taurus are:

"Let struggle be undismayed."
"I see and when the Eye is opened, all is light."[4]

Gemini, the Twins, guard the mystery of duality. Under the influences of the "Brothers who live in the Light," a person becomes increasingly aware of intuition. The light of the personality dims and the light of the soul waxes, and the personality becomes increasingly responsive to the soul impression. The light of interplay reveals the basic duality of manifestation and the relationship of spirit and form. This produces strain, action and reaction, and that condition of struggle and difficulty which is so characteristic of our planetary life. But it eventually produces the awakening of humanity to full planetary consciousness, and, in the case of the planetary Logos, to full cosmic consciousness.

The keynotes of the sign of Gemini are:

"Let instability do its work."
"I recognize my other self, and in the waning of that self, I grow and glow."[5]

Cancer, the Crab, is the sign that admits all souls as individual entities into human incarnation after they have first emerged as mental entities in Aries, as emotional entities in Taurus, and as vital entities in Gemini. Cancer is one of the great gates of the Zodiac, opening the door into human experience. Its keynote, indicating its purpose, is "I build a lighted house and therein dwell." The sign of Cancer enables a person to respond to contacts coming from all points of the compass, from every angle of the zodiacal wheel, and from that which is within as well as from that which is without.[6]

Leo, the Lion, is the sign of the self-conscious individual and of personality unfoldment. It is the sign wherein the consciousness of individuality is developed, utilised, and finally consecrated to divine purpose. Today, under the influence of Leo and due to the stress of circumstance and the results of certain events, thousands of men and women are stepping out of the deep sleep of irresponsiblity, becoming aware of themselves, and achieving integration of the personality. Individuals are gradually subordinating their integrated personality to the good of the group. The truly self-conscious person is one who is aware of purpose, of a self-directed life, and of a developed and definite life plan and program.

Leo is the constellation through which the will-to-fulfillment or to achievement pours into humanity and on to the planet.
The keynotes of the sign of Leo are:

"Let other forms exist. I rule because I am."
"I am That and That I am."[7]

Virgo, the Virgin Mother, is the sign that concerns the whole goal of the evolutionary process, which is to shield, nurture, and eventually reveal the hidden spiritual reality—the Christ-consciousness within. Its keynote is "Christ in you, the hope of glory." Virgo provides that which is needed for the mental, emotional, and physical expression of the hidden but ever present Divinity. She is the cosmic mother because she cosmically represents the negative pole to the positive father-spirit. In Virgo, the purpose for which life exists begins to be realised; and the desire for personality satisfaction begins to change. The recognition of the indwelling Christ assumes increasing control until the inner spiritual reality is eventually released from its bondage to matter and emerges in its own true nature.[8]

Libra, the Balance, guards the secret of balance and equilibrium, and it finally speaks the word that releases the initiate from the power of the Lord of Karma and admits the soul into the highest world center. It demonstrates the perfect balance of spirit and matter, which first came together in Aries. Libra occupies a unique place in the Great Wheel, for it is the energy coming forth from this constellation that controls the "hub of the wheel" where the twelve zodiacal energies meet and cross.

Libra lacks spectacular interest of any kind; it is a sign of balancing, of careful weighing of values, and it is the sign of intuitive perception. Libra governs the legal profession; law must become the custodian of a positive righteousness and not simply the instrument of enforcement. Its keynote for the spiritually awakened person is "I choose the way which leads between the two great lines of force." Libra is the light that oscillates until a point of balance is achieved; it provides a curious see-saw experience.[9]

Scorpio, the Scorpion, is under the influence of Sirius, the great star of initiation, and governs the path of discipleship in the human evolution. It influences the turning point from a spiritually unawakened state of being to spiritual awareness and cooperation in the life of humanity as well as in the life of the individual human being. With its tests and trials, Scorpio prepares the process of orientation to the life of the soul, readiness for initiation, and sensitivity to the Plan. It is the sign of tests, trials, and triumph. When the problems are solved by the reasoning mind, right relations with the soul and the environment result.

The keynote of Scorpio is triumph. After the first conscious steps toward group awareness and group response—plus group service—are taken, the desire to tread the Path of Return becomes so strong that regardless of pain and cost, the disciple discards old identifications; then new trends of higher, subtle, and more spiritual identification take hold. Ambition gives way to the executive activity of the soul, which transmutes personality desires into soul purpose. A Scorpio keyword is "Warrior I am and from the battle I emerge triumphant."

Scorpio is the sign wherein the Christ demonstrates His control over matter in the guise of the triumphant disciple. Scorpio—The Light of Day—is the place where three lights meet: the light of form, the light of soul, and the light of life. They meet, they blend, they rise.[10]

Sagittarius, the Archer, is the sign under which we direct our arrow toward a desired goal, reach that goal, and set another. Its keynote is ambition on the personality level and aspiration and direction on the soul level. The spiritually awakened person turns from ambition to aspiration, from selfishness to an intense desire to selflessness, from individual one-pointed self-interest to the one-pointedness of the disciple. The arrow of aspiration returns to the sender as the arrow of intuition that brings a person eventually to the foot of the mountain of initiation.

Sagittarius is powerfully affecting the world aspirants, leading them towards those attitudes of mind that will produce an unswerving allegiance to spiritual values and an unalterable adherence to the good of humanity. In this sign the "forces of conflict" are powerful; harmony through conflict is ceaselessly active and appears in outer and inner assignments. While at first ambition is directed to personality satisfaction, Sagittarian energy impels to ever more inclusive love-wisdom expression, which is selflessly developed and always concerns the good of the whole. The beam of light of Sagittarius reveals the greater light ahead and illumines the way to the source of Light.

The keynotes of Sagittarius are:

"Let food be sought."
"I see the goal. I reach that goal and then I see another."[11]

Capricorn, the Goat, is the most mysterious sign of all twelve. Aries, Taurus, and Capricorn are the great transformers under the creative plan. Each of them opens a door into one of the divine centres of expression. Capricorn opens the door into the life of the Spirit, into the life of the kingdom of God, the life and purposes of the Hierarchy of our planet. Its symbol is the mountaintop, after which a new cycle of effort is inaugurated. Capricorn admits the soul into conscious participation in the life of that world center we call the Hierarchy. It is a sign of extremes. A human being can express all the worst and all the best of which he or she is capable; it is the battleground of old established habits and the new and higher inclinations. In Capricorn there is full expression of the earthly nature, but there are also immense spiritual possibilities.

In Capricorn the initiate learns to realize the meaning of the growing light that greets his progress as he climbs up toward the mountaintop. The flashes of intuition change into the light of the soul, irradiating the mind until the light of the personality and the light of the soul blend and the Christ-consciousness, which is group-consciousness, controls. Capricorn, the transfiguring agent, will influence the will to release form life and enter the kingdom wherein the *will aspect* of Divinity expresses itself.

The keynotes of the sign of Capricorn are:

"Let ambition rule and let the door stand wide."
"Lost am I in light supernal, yet on that light I turn my back."[12]

Aquarius, the Water-Carrier, with its planetary rulers is of supreme importance to our solar system at this time as our Sun is rapidly moving into the influences of this sign with its all-pervasive yet often intangible outer effects. Under its influences the superficial, selfish activity of the personality changes to one of profound conviction and sensitive humanitarian awareness. The self-consciousness of Leo expands into the group-consciousness of Aquarius, and the individual human being becomes humanity itself, while yet preserving his spiritual identity.

The third Ray of Active Intelligence expresses itself powerfully through this sign, and the influences of the planets governing the decanates—Saturn, Mercury, Venus—are unusually potent during the present world cycle. Saturn is the planet of opportunity to destroy that which holds back the free expression of the soul. Mercury illumines our own mind to help us interpret the significance of events in the light of the soul. Venus—the union of heart and mind—will usher in the era of love-wisdom and expressed brotherly relationships. Opportunity, illumination, and brotherhood are gifts in store for us if we but prepare for them, accept them, and use them. The keynote of the sign of Aquarius is "Self-conscious living which changes finally into a sensitive humanitarian awareness."[13]

Pisces, the Fishes, stand symbolically for the soul and for the personality or form. The energies of this sign eventually fuse soul and form. Pisces produces the incarnated Christ, the perfected individual soul, the completed manifestation of the microcosm. Under the influences of Pisces, a person develops from the imprisonment of the soul in matter and form to where the soul is the prisoner of the personality. Then gradually the reversal takes place and the personality is brought under the control of the soul. Finally, the soul detaches itself from the personality and reattaches itself in consciousness to the ONE Who sent it forth.

Pisces carries the tests in Scorpio into the region of the mental processes, which is the reflection of the will aspect of Divinity. These tests carry the self-will of the personality up into the region of the divine will, and the result is inspiration and the emergence of a world savior. The keynote of the dual sign of Pisces is "transmutation"—from negativity into positive soul control, and from selfishness to divine selflessness.[14]

We can begin to see the tremendous, magnificent, interrelated, dynamic, and effective scheme of the Plan of God in which our solar system, our Earth, and we human beings play a part. The will of God, the love of God, hidden and latent in every living form becomes gradually revealed, alive, aware, and finally triumphant under the beneficently impelling energies that radiate into our life from the Seven Rays, the twelve constellations of the Zodiac, and our Sun and its planets as we respond to their reality and intent.

The nature of the soul or consciousness is light. This "growth of light in light" has been beautifully and symbolically hinted at in the following summarisation by D. K.:

ARIES *The Light of Life Itself.* This is the dim point of light found at the center of the cycle of manifestation, faint and flickering. It is the "searchlight of the Logos, seeking that which can be used" for divine expression.

TAURUS *The penetrating Light of the Path.* This is a beam of light streaming forth from the point in Aries, and revealing the area of light control.

GEMINI *The Light of Interplay.* This is a line of light beams, revealing that which opposes or the basic duality of manifestation, the relationship of spirit and of form. It is the conscious light of that relationship.

CANCER *The Light within the form.* This is the diffused light of substance itself, the "dark light" of matter, referred to in *The Secret Doctrine.* It is the light awaiting the stimulation coming from the soul light.

LEO *The Light of the Soul.* A reflected point of light logoic, or divine. The light diffused in Cancer focusses and reveals eventually a point.

VIRGO   *The blended dual Light.* Two lights are seen—bright and strong, the light of form; one faint and dim, the light of God. This light is distinguished by a waxing of one and the waning of the other. It differs from the light in Gemini.

LIBRA   *The Light that moves to rest.* This is the light that oscillates until a point of balance is achieved. It is the light that is distinguished by a moving up and down.

SCORPIO   *The Light of Day.* This is the place where three lights meet—the light of form, the light of soul, and the light of life. They meet; they blend; they rise.

SAGITTARIUS   *A beam of directed, focussed Light.* In this the point of light becomes the beam, revealing a greater light ahead and illumining the way to the center of the light.

CAPRICORN   *The Light of Initiation.* This is the light which clears the way to the mountain top, and produces transfiguration, thus revealing the rising sun.

AQUARIUS   *The Light that shines on Earth, across the sea.* This is the light which ever shines within the dark and cleansing with its healing rays that which must be purified until the dark has gone.

PISCES   *The Light of the World.* This is the light, revealing the light of life itself. It ends for ever the darkness of matter.[15]

NOTES

1. H. A. Rey, *The Stars: A New Way to See Them* (Boston: Houghton, Mifflin Co., 1967).
2. Ibid., pp. 141–42.
3. See *Esoteric Astrology*, pp. 93–107, 152, 329, 619.
4. Ibid., pp. 371–72, 488, 403.
5. Ibid., pp. 329, 357–58, 370.
6. Ibid., pp. 92, 168, 322, 654.
7. Ibid., pp. 196, 289–90, 311, 486, 619–20.
8. Ibid., pp. 251–52, 259–60.
9. Ibid., pp. 165–68, 183, 227–37, 251, 330.
10. Ibid., pp. 195–209, 220–26, 272, 330.
11. Ibid., pp. 118–21, 175–229, 193, 485.
12. Ibid., pp. 157–81, 265–66, 620–26.
13. Ibid., pp. 134–38, 153.
14. Ibid., pp. 115–34, 205, 123, 124.
15. Ibid., pp. 328–33.

References

Bailey, Alice A. *A Treatise on Cosmic Fire* (New York: Lucis Publishing Co.)

———. *A Treatise on White Magic* (New York: Lucis Publishing Co.)

———. *Destiny of the Nations* (New York: Lucis Publishing Co.)

———. *Esoteric Astrology* (New York: Lucis Publishing Co.)

———. *Esoteric Psychology*, vols. I and II (New York: Lucis Publishing Co.)

———. *Glamour, a World Problem* (New York: Lucis Publishing Co.)

———. *Reappearance of the Christ* (New York: Lucis Publishing Co.)

———. *The Rays and the Initiations* (New York: Lucis Publishing Co.)

Hall, Manly P. *The Space Born* (Los Angeles: Philosophical Research Society).

Leadbeater, C. W. *The Chakras* (Chicago: Theosophical Press).

National Geographic, May 1974 (Washington, D.C.: National Geographic Society).

Rey, H. A. *The Stars* (Boston: Houghton Mifflin Co.).

Szent-Györgyi, A. *The Physical Basis of Life* (Del Mar, Calif.: CRM Books).

World Goodwill (New York: Lucis Trust).

Twenty-four Books of Esoteric Philosophy

by
Alice A. Bailey

Published by The Lucis Publishing Company

The Unfinished Autobiography
Although her death in December 1949 prevented the completion of this book, enough of the author's life story emerges to show the stages in her journey from Christian evangelism to mastery of the science of esotericism, author, lecturer and teacher.

The Consciousness of the Atom
In this book the scientific relation of *matter* and *consciousness* is discussed as evolution progressively affects the atomic substance of all forms. The "atom" emerges as a miniature but complete replica of the energy structure common to all forms of life —cosmic, planetary, human and subhuman.

The Destiny of the Nations
A nation is an evolving spiritual entity, subject, as a man is, to the impact of energies. These energies influence the national consciousness, encouraging recognition of soul destiny and cooperation with that evolving process. The spiritual destiny of many nations and their predisposing soul and personality influences are discussed in this book.

Discipleship in the New Age, Volumes I and II

These two volumes contain the record of a series of personal and group instructions given to a small group of aspirants over a period of fifteen years by a Master of the Wisdom. They contain detailed teachings on Meditation, Initiation and the Six Stages of Discipleship. They emphasise the new age, pioneering necessity for group work, the development of group consciousness, and the change in training for initiation from individuals to discipleship *groups.*

Education in the New Age

Education should be a continuous process from birth to death. It is essentially a process leading to reconciliation of the human and divine elements in the constitution of a human being. Right relationship between God and man, spirit and matter, the whole and the part, should be a prime objective of educational techniques.

The Externalisation of the Hierarchy

This book discusses the interdependence of all states of consciousness and kingdoms in nature within the planet. It shows the interaction between humanity, the Hierarchy and Shamballa, and sets out the essentials of Plan and Purpose which influence human affairs. The process of the externalisation of certain ashrams within the Hierarchy and the practical effects of the process are given in detail.

From Bethlehem to Calvary

The life experience of the Master Jesus, including the Crucifixion, the Great Renunciation, is reflected in the life experience of all human beings. We can know and consciously cooperate in the journey which leads from the place of spiritual birth to the place of renunciation and resurrection.

From Intellect to Intuition

The development of the intellect, while necessary, is a means to an end. The intellect should become a means of penetrating into

122

new dimensions of thought and consciousness, and of awakening the intuitive faculty of "pure reason". Through occult meditation the gap is bridged between the threefold mind and the intuition.

Glamour: A World Problem

World glamour—the sum total of human ignorance, fear and greed—can dissipate through the clear, inclusive thinking of those in whom the soul (Christ) principle is awakening. Glamour results from a negative emotional focus; the dissipation of glamour depends on "illumined thinking".

Initiation, Human and Solar

An initiation is an expansion of consciousness, leading to revelation and illumination. Initiation is experienced by all forms of life, great and small. The work of the planetary Hierarchy, in its many stages of Mastership, is outlined in this book, and the Fourteen Rules are given by which the neophyte may become an Applicant at the Portal of Initiation.

The Light of the Soul

This volume is an original paraphrase, with commentary, of the Yoga Sutras of Patanjali. The Yoga Sutras are of ancient origin, first reduced to writing by Patanjali, who is considered the founder of the Raja Yoga School. Control of the mind and its illumination by the soul are brought about through the practice of Raja Yoga.

Letters on Occult Meditation

The science of meditation, as a mind-training technique, is increasingly practiced everywhere. Meditation is concerned with energy flow, energy which is impersonal and fiery in nature; its potential dangers should therefore be understood and avoided, and practices adopted which are safe and trustworthy. This book sets out the basic factors, general and specific, showing the overall objective of the science of meditation to be *planetary service.*

123

Problems of Humanity

Six basic world problems, with many ramifications, continue to present humanity with opportunity for progress. A perspective on these problems is shown in this book; the spiritual factors and subjective causes are related to the outer appearances and effects on the world scene.

The Reappearance of the Christ

Many religions today expect the coming of an Avatar or Saviour. The second coming of the Christ, as the world Teacher for the age of Aquarius, is presented in this book as an imminent event, logical and practical in the continuity of divine revelation throughout the ages. The Christ belongs to all mankind; he can be known and understood as "the same great Identity in all the world religions".

The Soul and Its Mechanism

The soul works through the mechanism of the threefold personality. The method by which the soul and the personality vehicles interact and function together is presented in this volume; and also the way the human constitution, as a whole and in its component parts, responds to the impact of an evolving consciousness.

Telepathy and the Etheric Vehicle

The scientific basis for the widely accepted ideal of the "brotherhood of man" rests on the fact of the interwoven etheric—or energy—structure underlying all forms in all kingdoms within the planet. It is this essential oneness which provides the conditions for intercommunication on all levels of consciousness, and creates the possibility of simultaneous impression in many by a stream of Plan-inspired energy.

A Treatise on Cosmic Fire

This volume deals with the underlying structure of occult teaching for the present era and with those vast cosmic processes reproduced through all areas of life from universe to atom. A large section of the book is directed to a detailed exposition of Solar Fire, the Fire of Mind, since this is the dominant energy to be understood and controlled during this second solar system. Among other values, the book provides a compact outline of a scheme of cosmology, philosophy and psychology which serves as a basic reference and text book.

A Treatise on the Seven Rays:
Esoteric Psychology, Volumes I and II

Five volumes have been written under the overall title of *A Treatise on the Seven Rays*, based on the fact, the nature, the quality and the interrelationship of the seven streams of energy pervading our solar system, our planet and all that lives and moves within its orbit. These two volumes go extensively into the psychological make-up of a human being as the life, quality and appearance of an incarnating, evolving spiritual entity. They also relate the circumstance of a human psychology to world conditions and to future possibilities.

Esoteric Astrology, Volume III

The science of esoteric astrology is said to be the basic occult science of the future. Astrology is described in this book as "the science of relationships", a science which deals with those conditioning energies and forces which play through and upon the whole field of space and all that is found within it.

Esoteric Healing, Volume IV

Healing is an exact and an exacting science. Esoteric healing is equally scientific, based on a number of requirements, including knowledge of the constitution of man as a spiritual being and of the biology and anatomy of his physical form. In this book the seven ray techniques of healing are described; the laws and rules of healing are discussed; basic causes of disease are shown; and requirements for healing are given in detail.

The Rays and the Initiations, Volume V
The first part of this volume contains the Fourteen Rules for Group Initiation, an extension of the teachings given in *Initiation, Human and Solar* on the Fourteen Rules for Applicants. The second part of the book is concerned with the nine initiations by which the disciple progressively liberates himself from the various forms of our planetary life. The possibility of group initiation is a development of the present era; this volume emphasises the growth of the group idea—group service, group responsibility, group initiation and group absorption into the centre Hierarchy.

A Treatise on White Magic
This book contains the Fifteen Rules for Magic (for soul control)—the soul, the White Magician, becoming manifest through its own inherent "magical" powers. Man is essentially and inherently divine. The soul is the means whereby mankind evolves a *consciousness* of divinity, redeems gross matter and liberates the pure flame of spirit from the limitation of form.

All Alice Bailey's books are available in clothbound and paperback editions. An up-to-date price list is available on request from the LUCIS PUBLISHING COMPANY, 113 University Place, 11th Floor, New York, N.Y. 10003.